BOB DYLAN THE LYRICS 1961—2020

# A HARD RAIN'S
# A-GONNA FALL
# 暴雨将至

**鲍勃·迪伦诗歌集 1961—2020**
VOL.01

[美] 鲍勃·迪伦 著　李皖 译

中信出版集团 | 北京

图书在版编目（CIP）数据

鲍勃·迪伦诗歌集：1961—2020：英汉对照/
（美）鲍勃·迪伦著；李皖，顾悦译．-- 北京：中信出
版社，2024.10
书名原文：The Lyrics: 1961-2020
ISBN 978-7-5217-5820-7

I. ①鲍…　II. ①鲍…②李…③顾…　III. ①诗集−
美国−现代−英、汉　IV. ① I712.25

中国国家版本馆 CIP 数据核字 (2023) 第 134968 号

鲍勃·迪伦诗歌集 1961—2020（英汉对照）
著者：　　　[美] 鲍勃·迪伦
译者：　　　李皖　顾悦
出版发行：中信出版集团股份有限公司
　　　　　（北京市朝阳区东三环北路 27 号嘉铭中心　邮编　100020）
承印者：　河北鹏润印刷有限公司

开本：787mm×1092mm　1/32　　　印张：70.75　　　字数：700 千字
版次：2024 年 10 月第 1 版　　　印次：2024 年 10 月第 1 次印刷
京权图字：01-2023-1172　　　　　书号：ISBN 978-7-5217-5820-7
　　　　　　　　　定价：298.00 元（全十册）

版权所有·侵权必究
如有印刷、装订问题，本公司负责调换。
服务热线：400-600-8099
投稿邮箱：author@citicpub.com

# 鲍勃·迪伦
## BOB DYLAN

## 自由不羁的鲍勃·迪伦
### *THE FREEWHEELIN' BOB DYLAN*

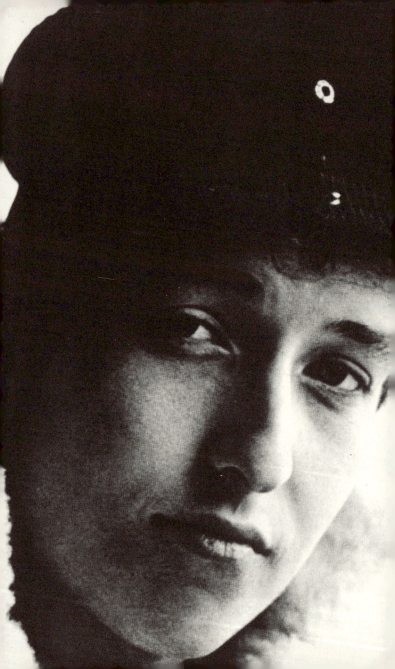

# BOB DYLAN
# 鲍勃 · 迪伦

说说纽约

献给伍迪的歌

附加歌词 ─────────────────────

纽约城的苦日子

谈熊山野餐惨案蓝调

流浪赌徒威利

站在公路上

穷孩子蓝调

给一位友人的歌谣

街上的人

埃米特 · 蒂尔之死

让我死在我的脚步里

宝贝，我在想你

很久以前，很远的地方

不会哀悼

吉卜赛阿露

用很长时间走

沿路走下去

旅行火车

唐纳德 · 怀特之歌

戒掉你的低劣行径

我真不想在那个可怕的日子成为你

纠结的困惑

英雄蓝调

明天是一段漫长的时光

鲍勃 · 迪伦的新奥尔良拉格

全是因为你

约翰 · 布朗

告别

Big City Blues by Bob Dylan 1961

I been thinkin' a out you darlin'
You been on my mind
But i cant stay long in this here town
I ain't the settlin' kind
Rain is crashin on the roof
My boots ~~are soggy wet~~ feel hot as coals
Got to keep movin' on
You know i got to go

Goin' to New York city
Gonna find my way
Gonna play in the biggest nightclu
underneath the lights of ol'Broadway
Heard lots a things about that big town
Heard the streets are ~~b~~ full of gold
Gonna dig me up a brick take it to the bank
gonna roll, jelly roll

1941 年 5 月 24 日，罗伯特·艾伦·齐默尔曼（Robert Allen Zimmerman）出生于明尼苏达州德卢斯，在希宾市一个铁矿小城长大。10 岁时他自学了钢琴，随后又学会了吉他和口琴。他学业成绩不突出，但酷爱读书、听音乐，在一家家电台和一间间唱片店费力地搜求着那些带来了新信息的声音。他原本钟情于新兴起的潮流——摇滚乐和电声布鲁斯，在高中时组建和加入了几个校园乐队。

　　1959 年 9 月，齐默尔曼离开希宾，去往明尼阿波利斯就读于明尼苏达大学艺术系，在这里，接触了正在复兴的美国民歌。这年底，他从朋友那里第一次听到了伍迪·格思里（Woody Guthrie）的老唱片，大地仿佛裂开了，他的头开始眩晕。那天，他一整个下午都在听格思里的歌，感觉自己"正处于世界的内部，发现了自我控制的本质——格思里的歌包含了全人类所有的感情。"[1]

　　1960 年冬，19 岁的齐默尔曼离开故乡，只身来到纽约，在格林尼治村的民谣俱乐部卖唱，给自己取名鲍

---

[1]　见迪伦自传《像一块滚石：鲍勃·迪伦回忆录第一卷》，徐振锋、吴宏凯译，南京：江苏人民出版社，2006 年，第 235—236 页。（除特殊说明，本书注释均为译者注。）

勃·迪伦。一年多的时间里他居无定所，只能在新结识朋友家客厅的沙发上蹭睡。靠着演出积攒的口碑，次年，迪伦认识了极有名望的制作人约翰·H.哈蒙德（John H. Hammond），与哥伦比亚唱片公司签下了5年合约。

1962年3月19日，鲍勃·迪伦同名专辑，也是首张录音室专辑《鲍勃·迪伦》，由哥伦比亚唱片公司发行。专辑中只有两首原创作品，《说说纽约》和《献给伍迪的歌》；另外11首曲目，为迪伦翻唱的经典民歌、布鲁斯和美国传统歌曲。本书除了收入《说说纽约》和《献给伍迪的歌》，也将26首写于这一时期的迪伦早期之作，作为"附加歌词"编入了这一辑。

据迪伦时任女友苏西·罗托洛的姐姐卡拉说："他（迪伦）大部分时间都在听我的唱片，夜以继日。他研究了《'民谣之路'美国民间音乐选集》（Folkways Anthology of American Folk Music），埃万·麦科尔（Ewan MacColl）和A. L.劳埃德（A. L. Lloyd）的演唱，'兔子'布朗（Rabbit Brown）的吉他演奏，格思里，当然还有布鲁斯……他的唱片正在计划阶段。我们都关心迪伦要录什么。我清楚地记得谈过这件事。"

这张专辑只于1961年11月20、22日在哥伦比亚第七大道录音室录了两个下午，各3小时。哈蒙德后来开玩笑说，哥伦比亚唱片公司统共只花了"大约402美元"。以如此短的录音时间和如此少的制作成本，即做出了这样的一张专辑，这成了迪伦的一个传奇。

但据哈蒙德说，录音其实不容易。"鲍比爆破每一个'p'音，嘶响每一个's'音，并会习惯性地偏离麦克风……更令人沮丧的是，他拒绝从错误中吸取教训。我当时想，我还从未与这么不规矩的人合作过呢。"在录音期间，迪伦还拒绝重录，"我说不。我不能想象自己把同一首歌连着唱两遍。那太可怕了。"

26首早期之作，绝大多数曾选编于《靴子腿系列第9辑·威特马克小样：1962—1964》(*The Bootleg Series Vol. 9: The Witmark Demos: 1962–1964*)，于2010年由哥伦比亚唱片公司出版。

迪伦这些最早期的作品，展现了他虽年纪轻轻，却有着深深沉浸于民歌、布鲁斯、乡村与西部音乐等美国传统音乐的自觉。他从聆听这些歌曲入手，建构起自己的音乐体系。当时，这类作品大多很难找，需四处搜寻、向人借阅。迪伦学习和借鉴它们的体裁和内容，包括诗歌与歌曲的形式、语言、意象、修辞、韵律、旋律、节奏等等，当然也包括在演唱上从布鲁斯音乐借来的如民间老人一般的苍凉嗓音，由此，迪伦获得了远超他年龄的智慧。虽然这些歌曲大多是习作，很快被迪伦抛于脑后，未收入正式专辑，其形式上却普遍有一股清新与纯正。从文学上看，迪伦早早即站在了美国民歌传统的制高点上。

以这张处女专辑，迪伦态度鲜明地表示，美国音乐的未来必须立足于前辈大师的音乐遗产之上，无论是白人的还是黑人的。如专辑中一首歌名所示，他从此成为一个"永远悲伤的人"，被世界的动荡、混乱和不公正困扰，思索着人世间的苦难、不平、黑暗以及死亡。这张专辑虽然在美国仅售出5000张，却在年轻人中获得了广泛共鸣，也得到一些黑人老布鲁斯艺人的赞赏。

## TALKING NEW YORK

Ramblin' outa the wild West
Leavin' the towns I love the best
Thought I'd seen some ups and downs
'Til I come into New York town
People goin' down to the ground
Buildings goin' up to the sky

Wintertime in New York town
The wind blowin' snow around
Walk around with nowhere to go
Somebody could freeze right to the bone
I froze right to the bone
New York Times said it was the coldest winter in seventeen years
I didn't feel so cold then

I swung onto my old guitar
Grabbed hold of a subway car
And after a rocking, reeling, rolling ride
I landed up on the downtown side
Greenwich Village

I walked down there and ended up

## 说说纽约

流浪过狂野西部
离开我至爱的城市
自以为见过了一些起伏
直到我来到了纽约城
人们往地下走
楼都往天上去

纽约城的冬天
风吹雪片处处
到处走可是无处去
有人会冷得入骨
我冷得入骨
《纽约时报》说这是十七年来最冷的冬日
让我觉得没那么冷了

旧吉他在身上荡
抢上一节地铁车厢
历经摇晃、旋转和翻滚
我着陆在市中心边上
格林尼治村

我在那儿走，最后走进

In one of them coffee-houses on the block

Got on the stage to sing and play

Man there said, "Come back some other day

You sound like a hillbilly

We want folk singers here"

Well, I got a harmonica job, begun to play

Blowin' my lungs out for a dollar a day

I blowed inside out and upside down

The man there said he loved m' sound

He was ravin' about how he loved m' sound

Dollar a day's worth

And after weeks and weeks of hangin' around

I finally got a job in New York town

In a bigger place, bigger money too

Even joined the union and paid m' dues

Now, a very great man once said

That some people rob you with a fountain pen

其中一家街区咖啡馆

走上台又唱又弹

那边那人说："改日再来吧

你听着像个乡巴佬

我们要的是民谣歌手"


好吧，我找到了吹口琴的差事，开始吹

吹得肺爆一天一美元

我吹得里外翻转上下颠倒

那边那人说他好喜欢

他不停吹他多爱这琴声

一天一美元值了


几星期几星期就这么过去

终于我在纽约城找到了工作

场子大些，钱也多些

甚至加入工会缴了会费


喏，一个很伟大的人说过

有人用钢笔抢劫 [1]

---

[1] "一个很伟大的人说过 / 有人用钢笔抢劫"，参考伍迪·格思里的《帅哥弗洛伊德》（"Pretty Boy Floyd"），其中有段歌词是："当我漫游过这世界，/ 我见过许多有趣的人；/ 有的人用六发左轮抢劫，/ 有的人用钢笔。"迪伦这首歌的结构和主题与格思里的《说说哥伦比亚》（"Talkin' Columbia"）和《说说地铁》（"Talkin' Subway"）有一定的关联。

It didn't take too long to find out

Just what he was talkin' about

A lot of people don't have much food on their table

But they got a lot of forks 'n' knives

And they gotta cut somethin'

So one mornin' when the sun was warm

I rambled out of New York town

Pulled my cap down over my eyes

And headed out for the western skies

So long, New York

Howdy, East Orange

没多久我就明白了
这句话是何用意
许多人的桌上都没多少食物
但他们有许多刀叉
他们必须切些东西

于是一天早晨，当太阳变暖
我漫步走出纽约城
把帽子拉下来遮住双眼
然后走向那西部天边
别了，纽约
你好，东奥兰治

# SONG TO WOODY

I'm out here a thousand miles from my home
Walkin' a road other men have gone down
I'm seein' your world of people and things
Your paupers and peasants and princes and kings

Hey, hey, Woody Guthrie, I wrote you a song
'Bout a funny ol' world that's a-comin' along
Seems sick an' it's hungry, it's tired an' it's torn
It looks like it's a-dyin' an' it's hardly been born

Hey, Woody Guthrie, but I know that you know
All the things that I'm a-sayin' an' a-many times more
I'm a-singin' you the song, but I can't sing enough
'Cause there's not many men that done the things that you've
    done

Here's to Cisco an' Sonny an' Leadbelly too

## 献给伍迪的歌 [1]

离家一千英里我来到这里
走在别人走过的路上
我在目睹你世界中的人和事
你的穷人与农民，王子与国王

嗨嗨，伍迪·格思里，我给你写了首歌
关于一个正走来的有趣的旧世界
似乎它病了，又饿又累而且又破
看上去快死了可是还没出生

嗨，伍迪·格思里，但我知道你知道
所有我正在说的事，而且还要多得多
我正在为你唱这首歌，可是我没法唱尽
因为没多少人做过你做过的
　　事情

这首歌也献给西斯科、桑尼和铅肚皮 [2]

---

[1]　此歌献给美国民歌复兴运动的巨匠伍迪·格思里（1912—1967），
　　旋律上借鉴了格思里的歌曲《1913 年的屠杀》（"1913 Massacre"）。
[2]　西斯科·休斯敦、桑尼·特里和铅肚皮，均为格思里的朋友，美国
　　知名民谣歌手。

An' to all the good people that traveled with you

Here's to the hearts and the hands of the men

That come with the dust and are gone with the wind

I'm a-leavin' tomorrow, but I could leave today

Somewhere down the road someday

The very last thing that I'd want to do

Is to say I've been hittin' some hard travelin' too

以及所有与你同行的好人
献给这些人的心灵与双手
他们随尘土而来又随风而去

我明天就离开，也可能今天就走
某天某地沿那条路走下去
我想做的最后一件事
是说我也走过了艰难旅途

# HARD TIMES IN NEW YORK TOWN

Come you ladies and you gentlemen, a-listen to my song
Sing it to you right, but you might think it's wrong
Just a little glimpse of a story I'll tell
'Bout an East Coast city that you all know well
It's hard times in the city
Livin' down in New York town

Old New York City is a friendly old town
From Washington Heights to Harlem on down
There's a-mighty many people all millin' all around
They'll kick you when you're up and knock you when you're
    down
It's hard times in the city
Livin' down in New York town

It's a mighty long ways from the Golden Gate
To Rockefeller Plaza 'n' the Empire State
Mister Rockefeller sets up as high as a bird
Old Mister Empire never says a word
It's hard times from the country
Livin' down in New York town

## 纽约城的苦日子

来吧女士们先生们，来听听我的歌
我唱给你的是对的，但你可能认为错了
我只讲一丁点儿
你们都熟悉的东海岸城市的故事
城里日子不好过
住在这纽约城里

老纽约是座友善的旧城
从华盛顿高地一直到哈莱姆区
都有巨量的人群穿来穿去
你起来时他们踢你，下去时他们
　　踩你
城里日子不好过
住在这纽约城里

那是一段超远的路，从金门大桥
到洛克菲勒中心和帝国大厦
洛克菲勒先生高高在上像只鸟
帝国老先生总是一言不发
乡下来的日子不好过
住在这纽约城里

Well, it's up in the mornin' tryin' to find a job of work

Stand in one place till your feet begin to hurt

If you got a lot o' money you can make yourself merry

If you only got a nickel, it's the Staten Island Ferry

And it's hard times in the city

Livin' down in New York town


Mister Hudson come a-sailin' down the stream

And old Mister Minuet paid for his dream

Bought your city on a one-way track

'F I had my way I'd sell it right back

And it's hard times in the city

Livin' down in New York town


I'll take all the smog in Cal-i-for-ne-ay

'N' every bit of dust in the Oklahoma plains

'N' the dirt in the caves of the Rocky Mountain mines

It's all much cleaner than the New York kind

And it's hard times in the city

Livin' down in New York town

好吧，早晨起来试着找工作

在一个地方站到脚疼

若有大把钱你就能自己乐

若只挣一个钢镚儿，那就得坐斯塔滕岛渡轮 [1]

城里日子不好过

住在这纽约城里


哈得孙先生 [2] 顺河航行

而小步舞老先生 [3] 花钱买梦

买下了你的城没有回头路

如果我做主我会转手卖出去

城里日子不好过

住在这纽约城里


我将会忍受加利福尼亚的所有雾霾

和俄克拉何马平原上的每颗沙尘

以及落基山矿山山洞里的土灰

这一切都比纽约的空气干净

城里日子不好过

住在这纽约城里

---

[1] 斯塔滕岛渡轮，斯塔滕岛与曼哈顿间的渡轮，票价五美分，属纽约
    城中这段路程最便宜的公共交通工具。

[2] 哈得孙，英国探险家，哈得孙河即得名于他。

[3] 小步舞老先生，指彼德·米纽伊特，17 世纪从印第安人手中买下了
    曼哈顿岛。

So all you newsy people, spread the news around

You c'n listen to m' story, listen to m' song

You c'n step on my name, you c'n try 'n' get me beat

When I leave New York, I'll be standin' on my feet

And it's hard times in the city

Livin' down in New York town

所以你们这些爱传事儿的人，把这事儿传出去
你可以听我的故事，听听我的歌
可以踩踏我的名字，可以给我一顿揍
等我离开了纽约，我将会靠自己独立
城里日子不好过
住在这纽约城里

## TALKING BEAR MOUNTAIN PICNIC MASSACRE BLUES

I saw it advertised one day
Bear Mountain picnic was comin' my way
"Come along 'n' take a trip
We'll bring you up there on a ship
Bring the wife and kids
Bring the whole family"
Yippee!

Well, I run right down 'n' bought a ticket
To this Bear Mountain Picnic
But little did I realize
I was in for a picnic surprise
Had nothin' to do with mountains
I didn't even come close to a bear

Took the wife 'n' kids down to the pier
Six thousand people there
Everybody had a ticket for the trip

## 谈熊山野餐惨案蓝调 [1]

有一天我看到广告
说熊山野餐的时间到了
"来吧去出游啊
我们会带你坐船过去
带上老婆孩子
带上全家"
太好啦!

于是，我直接跑去买票
去熊山野餐的票
可我万万没想到
会碰上野餐意外
跟山毫无关系
我甚至也没靠近熊

带老婆孩子到了码头
那儿聚了有六千人
人手一张野餐船票

---

[1] 1961 年 6 月 18 日，在沿哈得孙河坐船到纽约市北部熊山州立公园
的郊游中，有人卖假票，导致乘客太多，游船不胜负荷沉没，造成
多人死伤。

"Oh well," I said, "it's a pretty big ship
Besides, anyway, the more the merrier"

Well, we all got on 'n' what d'ya think
That big old boat started t' sink
More people kept a-pilin' on
That old ship was a-slowly goin' down
Funny way t' start a picnic

Well, I soon lost track of m' kids 'n' wife
So many people there I never saw in m' life
That old ship sinkin' down in the water
Six thousand people tryin' t' kill each other
Dogs a-barkin', cats a-meowin'
Women screamin', fists a-flyin', babies cryin'
Cops a-comin', me a-runnin'
Maybe we just better call off the picnic

I got shoved down 'n' pushed around
All I could hear there was a screamin' sound
Don't remember one thing more
Just remember wakin' up on a little shore
Head busted, stomach cracked
Feet splintered, I was bald, naked . . .
Quite lucky to be alive though

"噢好吧，"我说，"相当大的船啊
再说了，反正人越多越乐呵"

哎呀，哪承想我们一上去
那艘大旧船就开始沉
更多的人还在往上挤
那旧船慢慢沉没
野餐这开头有点儿怪异

哎呀，没多久孩子老婆都失去踪影
我一辈子没见过这么多人
旧船在水中下沉
六千人拼命自相残杀
狗汪汪叫，猫喵喵喵
女人尖叫，拳头呼啸，婴儿哭号
条子跑来，我也跑
也许这场野餐最好取消

我被挤来挤去挤倒了
只听到一片喧嚷
其他的都不记得了
只记得醒来在岸上
头破了，肚子撞了
脚划开了，身上赤条条了……
但是很幸运还活着

Feelin' like I climbed outa m' casket
I grabbed back hold of m' picnic basket
Took the wife 'n' kids 'n' started home
Wishin' I'd never got up that morn

Now, I don't care just what you do
If you wanta have a picnic, that's up t' you
But don't tell me about it, I don't wanta hear it
'Cause, see, I just lost all m' picnic spirit
Stay in m' kitchen, have m' own picnic . . .
In the bathroom

Now, it don't seem to me quite so funny
What some people are gonna do f'r money
There's a bran' new gimmick every day
Just t' take somebody's money away
I think we oughta take some o' these people
And put 'em on a boat, send 'em up to Bear Mountain . . .
For a picnic

感觉就像从棺材里爬出来
我紧抓着野餐篮子
带着老婆孩子动身返家
真希望那天早上我没起床

现在，你做什么我都无所谓
如果你要去野餐，那么悉听尊便
只是别跟我说，我不想听到
因为，你看，我完全失去了野餐的心境
只想待在厨房，自己办野餐……
在浴室里

喏，这对我来说并不好笑
有些人会为了钱搞事
每一天都有新花招
只为了弄走别人的钱
我想我们该把这些人弄走
把他们装上船，送上熊山……
去野餐

# RAMBLING, GAMBLING WILLIE

Come around you rovin' gamblers and a story I will tell
About the greatest gambler, you all should know him well
His name was Will O'Conley and he gambled all his life
He had twenty-seven children, yet he never had a wife
And it's ride, Willie, ride
Roll, Willie, roll
Wherever you are a-gamblin' now, nobody really knows

He gambled in the White House and in the railroad yards
Wherever there was people, there was Willie and his cards
He had the reputation as the gamblin'est man around
Wives would keep their husbands home when Willie came to
    town
And it's ride, Willie, ride
Roll, Willie, roll
Wherever you are a-gamblin' now, nobody really knows

Sailin' down the Mississippi to a town called New Orleans
They're still talkin' about their card game on that Jackson River
    Queen
"I've come to win some money," Gamblin' Willie says
When the game finally ended up, the whole damn boat was his

## 流浪赌徒威利

来吧，你们这些流浪赌徒，我来讲个故事
关于最大的赌徒，你们应该都很熟
他叫威尔·奥康利，赌了一辈子
儿女二十七个，却没有老婆
下注啊，威利，下注
掷骰子，威利，掷骰子
现在不管你在哪儿赌，没人真的知道

他在白宫赌，也在火车站场赌
哪儿有人，哪儿就有威利和他的牌
到处都在传他赌王的名声
威利进城时，妻子都会把丈夫看在
　家里
下注啊，威利，下注
掷骰子，威利，掷骰子
现在不管你在哪儿赌，没人真的知道

沿密西西比河坐船到了叫新奥尔良的城
他们还在谈论"杰克逊皇后"号上的
　赌局
"我是来赢钱的。"赌徒威利说
当赌局终于落定，该死的整条船都是他的

And it's ride, Willie, ride

Roll, Willie, roll

Wherever you are a-gamblin' now, nobody really knows


Up in the Rocky Mountains in a town called Cripple Creek

There was an all-night poker game, lasted about a week

Nine hundred miners had laid their money down

When Willie finally left the room, he owned the whole damn
    town

And it's ride, Willie, ride

Roll, Willie, roll

Wherever you are a-gamblin' now, nobody really knows


But Willie had a heart of gold and this I know is true

He supported all his children and all their mothers too

He wore no rings or fancy things, like other gamblers wore

He spread his money far and wide, to help the sick and the
    poor

And it's ride, Willie, ride

Roll, Willie, roll

Wherever you are a-gamblin' now, nobody really knows


When you played your cards with Willie, you never really
    knew

Whether he was bluffin' or whether he was true

He won a fortune from a man who folded in his chair

下注啊，威利，下注
掷骰子，威利，掷骰子
现在不管你在哪儿赌，没人真的知道


落基山脉有个小镇叫瘸子溪
有差不多一礼拜天天都有通宵牌局
九百个矿工拿出钱下注
当威利终于离开房间，他拥有了整个
　　该死的镇子
下注啊，威利，下注
掷骰子，威利，掷骰子
现在不管你在哪儿赌，没人真的知道


但是威利有一颗金子的心我知道这是真的
他养活他所有的孩子和孩子的母亲
他不戴戒指不穿华服，不像别的赌徒
他把钱财广为散发，帮助病人和
　　穷人
下注啊，威利，下注
掷骰子，威利，掷骰子
现在不管你在哪儿赌，没人真的知道


当你和威利玩牌时，你永远
　　不知道
他是在诈你还是真有好牌
他赢过一笔巨款，那人座上埋了牌

The man, he left a diamond flush, Willie didn't even have a pair

And it's ride, Willie, ride

Roll, Willie, roll

Wherever you are a-gamblin' now, nobody really knows


It was late one evenin' during a poker game

A man lost all his money, he said Willie was to blame

He shot poor Willie through the head, which was a tragic fate

When Willie's cards fell on the floor, they were aces backed
   with eights

And it's ride, Willie, ride

Roll, Willie, roll

Wherever you are a-gamblin' now, nobody really knows


So all you rovin' gamblers, wherever you might be

The moral of the story is very plain to see

Make your money while you can, before you have to stop

For when you pull that dead man's hand, your gamblin' days
   are up

And it's ride, Willie, ride

Roll, Willie, roll

Wherever you are a-gamblin' now, nobody really knows

扔掉了方块同花顺，而威利甚至没有对子
下注啊，威利，下注
掷骰子，威利，掷骰子
现在不管你在哪儿赌，没人真的知道


某个深夜在一场牌局的中途
一个输光了的人，说全是威利的错
他一枪击穿了可怜的威利的头，命运真是惨
威利的牌落在地上，面上对 A 手里
　　对八
下注啊，威利，下注
掷骰子，威利，掷骰子
现在不管你在哪儿赌，没人真的知道


所以你们这些流浪赌徒啊，不管你在哪儿
这个故事的寓意很显然
能赢则赢，在必须收手之前
因为当你抽到死人之手 [1]，赌博的日子
　　就到头了
下注啊，威利，下注
掷骰子，威利，掷骰子
现在不管你在哪儿赌，没人真的知道


[1]　死人之手，即诗中说到的"面上对 A 手里对八"。传说 1876 年在达
　　科他州戴德伍德一家酒馆，西部传奇枪手、赌徒詹姆斯·巴特勒·希
　　科克，被人从身后射杀，死时手里就是这副牌。

# STANDING ON THE HIGHWAY

Well, I'm standin' on the highway
Tryin' to bum a ride, tryin' to bum a ride
Tryin' to bum a ride
Well, I'm standin' on the highway
Tryin' to bum a ride, tryin' to bum a ride
Tryin' to bum a ride
Nobody seem to know me
Everybody pass me by

Well, I'm standin' on the highway
Tryin' to hold up, tryin' to hold up
Tryin' to hold up and be brave
Well, I'm standin' on the highway
Tryin' to hold up, tryin' to hold up and be brave
One road's goin' to the bright lights
The other's goin' down to my grave

Well, I'm lookin' down at two cards
They seem to be handmade
Well, I'm lookin' down at two cards
They seem to be handmade
One looks like it's the ace of diamonds

## 站在公路上

唉，我站在公路上
想搭个车，想搭个车
想搭个车
唉，我站在公路上
想搭个车，想搭个车
想搭个车
像是没人认识我
每人从我身边经过

唉，我站在公路上
尽力撑着，尽力撑着
尽力撑着并鼓足勇气
唉，我站在公路上
尽力撑着，尽力撑着并鼓足勇气
一条路通向灯火辉煌
另一条要下到我的墓地

唉，我低头看着两张牌
它们似乎是手工做的
唉，我低头看着两张牌
它们似乎是手工做的
一张看着像是方块 A

The other looks like it is the ace of spades

Well, I'm standin' on the highway
Watchin' my life roll by
Well, I'm standin' on the highway
Watchin' my life roll by
Well, I'm standin' on the highway
Tryin' to bum a ride

Well, I'm standin' on the highway
Wonderin' where everybody went,
   wonderin' where everybody went
Wonderin' where everybody went
Well, I'm standin' on the highway
Wonderin' where everybody went,
   wonderin' where everybody went
Wonderin' where everybody went
Please mister, pick me up
I swear I ain't gonna kill nobody's kids

I wonder if my good gal
I wonder if she knows I'm here
Nobody else seems to know I'm here
I wonder if my good gal
I wonder if she knows I'm here
Nobody else seems to know I'm here

另一张看着像是黑桃 A

唉，我站在公路上
望着我的生命流驶
唉，我站在公路上
望着我的生命流驶
唉，我站在公路上
想搭个车

唉，我站在公路上
好奇人都跑哪儿去了，
好奇人都跑哪儿去了
好奇人都跑哪儿去了
唉，我站在公路上
好奇人都跑哪儿去了，
好奇人都跑哪儿去了
好奇人都跑哪儿去了
劳烦您先生，带我一程吧
我发誓不会杀任何人的孩子

我在想我的好姑娘
我在想她知不知道我在这儿
别的人好像都不知道
我在想我的好姑娘
我在想她知不知道我在这儿
别的人好像都不知道

If she knows I'm here, Lawd
I wonder if she said a prayer

如果她知道我在这儿，上帝
我想知道她有没有在祈祷

## POOR BOY BLUES

Mm, tell mama
Where'd ya sleep last night?
Cain't ya hear me cryin'?
Hm, hm, hm

Hey, tell me baby
What's the matter here?
Cain't ya hear me cryin'?
Hm, hm, hm

Hey, stop you ol' train
Let a poor boy ride
Cain't ya hear me cryin'?
Hm, hm, hm

Hey, Mister Bartender
I swear I'm not too young
Cain't ya hear me cryin'?
Hm, hm, hm

Blow your whistle, policeman
My poor feet are trained to run

## 穷孩子蓝调

嗐，跟妈妈说
你昨晚去哪儿睡啦？
你听不见我哭吗？
嗯，嗯，嗯

诶，告诉我宝贝儿
出了什么事儿？
你听不见我哭吗？
嗯，嗯，嗯

诶，老火车你停一下
让穷孩子坐一程
你听不见我哭吗？
嗯，嗯，嗯

诶，调酒师先生
我发誓我不小了
你听不见我哭吗？
嗯，嗯，嗯

吹哨子的，警官大人
我可怜的脚被训练得乱跑

Cain't ya hear me cryin'?
Hm, hm, hm


Long-distance operator
I hear this phone call is on the house
Cain't ya hear me cryin'?
Hm, hm, hm


Ashes and diamonds
The diff'rence I cain't see
Cain't ya hear me cryin'?
Hm, hm, hm


Mister Judge and Jury
Cain't you see the shape I'm in?
Don't ya hear me cryin'?
Hm, hm, hm


Mississippi River
You a-runnin' too fast for me
Cain't ya hear me cryin'?
Hm, hm, hm

你听不见我哭吗？

嗯，嗯，嗯

长途接线员
我听说这通电话店家支付
你听不见我哭吗？
嗯，嗯，嗯

灰烬与钻石
我看不出来区别
你听不见我哭吗？
嗯，嗯，嗯

法官先生和陪审团
你们看不见我的样子吗？
你们听不见我哭吗？
嗯，嗯，嗯

密西西比河啊
我觉得你流得太快
你听不见我哭吗？
嗯，嗯，嗯

# BALLAD FOR A FRIEND

Sad I'm a-sittin' on the railroad track
Watchin' that old smokestack
Train is a-leavin' but it won't be back

Years ago we hung around
Watchin' trains roll through the town
Now that train is a-graveyard bound

Where we go up in that North Country
Lakes and streams and mines so free
I had no better friend than he

Something happened to him that day
I thought I heard a stranger say
I hung my head and stole away

A diesel truck was rollin' slow
Pullin' down a heavy load
It left him on a Utah road

They carried him back to his home town
His mother cried, his sister moaned
Listenin' to them church bells tone

## 给一位友人的歌谣

可怜我坐在铁轨上
望着那老烟囱
火车正离去它不会回程

多年前我们四处闲荡
望车轮滚滚穿过小镇
如今那火车却驶向坟场

我们北上去那北方
湖泊河流矿山空旷
他是我最好的死党

有一天他出了意外
我想我是听一个陌生人说的
我低下了头，悄悄走开

一辆柴油卡车开得很慢
拖着很重一车货
把他留在了犹他州路上

他们把他送归故里
他的母亲哭，他的妹妹悲泣
听着教堂的钟声响起

# MAN ON THE STREET

I'll sing you a song, ain't very long
'Bout an old man who never done wrong
How he died nobody can say
They found him dead in the street one day

Well, the crowd, they gathered one fine morn
At the man whose clothes 'n' shoes were torn
There on the sidewalk he did lay
They stopped 'n' stared 'n' walked their way

Well, the p'liceman come and he looked around
"Get up, old man, or I'm a-takin' you down"
He jabbed him once with his billy club
And the old man then rolled off the curb

Well, he jabbed him again and loudly said
"Call the wagon; this man is dead"
The wagon come, they loaded him in
I never saw the man again

I've sung you my song, it ain't very long
'Bout an old man who never done wrong

## 街上的人

我给你唱首歌，不很长
关于一个从不做坏事的老人
他是怎么死的没人讲得清
有一天他们发现他死在街上

哦，人群，一个美好的早晨他们聚集起来
围在那个衣服鞋子都破旧的男人周边
他确实是躺在人行道上
他们停下来盯一眼然后继续走路

哦，警察来了，他望望四周
"起来老头，不然我就把你带走"
他用警棍戳了他一下
老人就从路阶上滚下去

哦，他又戳了戳然后大声说
"叫马车，这人死了"
马车来了，他们把他装上车
我再没见过这个人

我的歌唱完了，不很长
关于一个从不做坏事的老人

How he died no one can say
They found him dead in the street one day

他是怎么死的没人讲得清
有一天他们发现他死在街上

# THE DEATH OF EMMETT TILL

'Twas down in Mississippi not so long ago

When a young boy from Chicago town stepped through a
   Southern door

This boy's dreadful tragedy I can still remember well

The color of his skin was black and his name was Emmett Till


Some men they dragged him to a barn and there they beat him
   up

They said they had a reason, but I can't remember what

They tortured him and did some things too evil to repeat

There were screaming sounds inside the barn,
   there were laughing sounds out on the street


Then they rolled his body down a gulf amidst a bloody red rain

And they threw him in the waters wide to cease his screaming
   pain

The reason that they killed him there, and I'm sure it ain't no lie

Was just for the fun of killin' him and to watch him slowly die

# 埃米特 · 蒂尔之死 [1]

此事发生在密西西比，不久前
当一个芝加哥来的少年走进南方一扇
　　宅门
这孩子的可怕遭遇我至今记忆犹新
他皮肤是黑的，名字是埃米特 · 蒂尔

几个人把他拖进了谷仓，在那儿
　　毒打他
他们说他们有理由，但我不记得那是什么
他们折磨他，干下了太邪恶而不能复述的事
谷仓里在惨叫，
　　外面街上有笑声

然后他们在血红的雨中将他滚下了河湾
接着把他扔进滔滔大水，结束他苦痛的
　　叫喊
他们之所以要在那儿害他，我敢肯定这真实不虚
只是为了取乐，杀掉他并看着他慢慢死去

---

[1] 1955 年 8 月 28 日，密西西比州金钱镇发生一桩惨案，两名白人杀
　　害了 14 岁少年埃米特 · 蒂尔，清一色的白人组成的陪审团却宣判
　　他们无罪。此案激发了 20 世纪 60 年代的美国民权运动。

And then to stop the United States of yelling for a trial

Two brothers they confessed that they had killed poor Emmett
Till

But on the jury there were men who helped the brothers
commit this awful crime

And so this trial was a mockery, but nobody seemed to mind


I saw the morning papers but I could not bear to see

The smiling brothers walkin' down the courthouse stairs

For the jury found them innocent and the brothers they went
free

While Emmett's body floats the foam of a Jim Crow southern
sea


If you can't speak out against this kind of thing, a crime that's
so unjust

Your eyes are filled with dead men's dirt, your mind is filled
with dust

Your arms and legs they must be in shackles and chains, and
your blood it must refuse to flow

For you let this human race fall down so God-awful low!

然后为了平息合众国审判的呼吁
两兄弟承认杀害了可怜的
　埃米特·蒂尔
但是陪审团中有人是两兄弟可怕
　罪行的帮凶
所以审判是个闹剧，但似乎没有人在意

我看了那天早上的报纸可是我不忍看
两兄弟微笑着走下法院的楼梯
陪审团认定他们无罪，所以两兄弟
　自由了
而埃米特的尸身还漂在南方吉姆·克劳 [1] 海的
　泡沫里

如果你不能大声反对这行径，这如此
　不公的审判
那么你的眼里塞满了死人污垢，你的
　心里飘满灰尘
你的手脚必受枷锁，你的血必拒绝
　流动
因为你让人类堕落到如此可怕的境地！

---

[1]　吉姆·克劳，黑奴代称。19 世纪美国白人黑面喜剧中的黑人角色叫
　　吉姆·克劳，遂名。1876—1965 年，美国南部各州对有色人种施
　　行一系列种族隔离法律，泛称吉姆·克劳法。

This song is just a reminder to remind your fellow man

That this kind of thing still lives today in that ghost-robed Ku
   Klux Klan

But if all of us folks that thinks alike, if we gave all we could
   give

We could make this great land of ours a greater place to live

这首歌只是提醒我们同胞的一份备忘
此类行径至今依然活在幽灵般的
　三K党身上
但是只要我们大家齐心，只要我们
　竭尽所能
我们就能让脚下的大地成为我们更好生活的地方

# LET ME DIE IN MY FOOTSTEPS

I will not go down under the ground
'Cause somebody tells me that death's comin' 'round
An' I will not carry myself down to die
When I go to my grave my head will be high
Let me die in my footsteps
Before I go down under the ground

There's been rumors of war and wars that have been
The meaning of life has been lost in the wind
And some people thinkin' that the end is close by
'Stead of learnin' to live they are learnin' to die
Let me die in my footsteps
Before I go down under the ground

I don't know if I'm smart but I think I can see
When someone is pullin' the wool over me
And if this war comes and death's all around
Let me die on this land 'fore I die underground
Let me die in my footsteps

## 让我死在我的脚步里 [1]

我不会走入地下
就因为有人告诉我说死亡将近
我不会让自己低头死
走向坟墓时我要高昂着头
让我死在我的脚步里
在我走入地下之前

到处是战争的风声和以前的战争
生命的意义已在风中飘逝
有人认为末日就在眼前
他们不学习生转而学习死
让我死在我的脚步里
在我走入地下之前

我不知道自己是否聪明，但我想有人蒙我时
我应该还看得清
如果这场战争真来了死亡无处不在
让我死在地上而非地下
让我死在我的脚步里

---

[1] 这首歌的背景是美苏冷战期间，美国修建了大量的防核尘地下工程，
并进行全民的防空袭演练。

Before I go down under the ground

There's always been people that have to cause fear
They've been talking of the war now for many long years
I have read all their statements and I've not said a word
But now Lawd God, let my poor voice be heard
Let me die in my footsteps
Before I go down under the ground

If I had rubies and riches and crowns
I'd buy the whole world and change things around
I'd throw all the guns and the tanks in the sea
For they are mistakes of a past history
Let me die in my footsteps
Before I go down under the ground

Let me drink from the waters where the mountain streams flood
Let the smell of wildflowers flow free through my blood
Let me sleep in your meadows with the green grassy leaves
Let me walk down the highway with my brother in peace
Let me die in my footsteps
Before I go down under the ground

Go out in your country where the land meets the sun
See the craters and the canyons where the waterfalls run
Nevada, New Mexico, Arizona, Idaho

在我走入地下之前

总是有人要制造恐怖
多年来他们一直在谈这场战争
我读了他们所有的论调我未置一词
但是现在上帝啊，让他们听见我可怜的声音
让我死在我的脚步里
在我走入地下之前

如果我有红宝石、财富和王冠
我就买下全世界然后将万物改变
我要把枪炮和坦克都丢进大海
因为它们是过去历史的错误
让我死在我的脚步里
在我走入地下之前

让我痛饮山涧喷涌的溪水
让野花香自由奔流在血液里
让我安睡在你碧叶青青的草场
让我和我的兄弟走在安宁的大路上
让我死在我的脚步里
在我走入地下之前

走进你的国家，那里大地与太阳相接
看那陨石坑和瀑布飞溅的峡谷
内华达、新墨西哥、亚利桑那、爱达荷

Let every state in this union seep down deep in your souls

And you'll die in your footsteps

Before you go down under the ground

让联邦的每一个州都浸入你灵魂的深处

而你将死在你的脚步里

在你走入地下之前

# BABY, I'M IN THE MOOD FOR YOU

Sometimes I'm in the mood, I wanna leave my lonesome home
And sometimes I'm in the mood, I wanna hear my milk cow
   moan
And sometimes I'm in the mood, I wanna hit that highway road
But then again, but then again, I said oh, I said oh, I said
Oh babe, I'm in the mood for you

Sometimes I'm in the mood, Lord, I had my overflowin' fill
Sometimes I'm in the mood, I'm gonna make out my final will
Sometimes I'm in the mood, I'm gonna head for the walkin' hill
But then again, but then again, I said oh, I said oh, I said
Oh babe, I'm in the mood for you

Sometimes I'm in the mood, I wanna lay right down and die
Sometimes I'm in the mood, I wanna climb up to the sky
Sometimes I'm in the mood, I'm gonna laugh until I cry
But then again, I said again, I said again, I said
Oh babe, I'm in the mood for you

Sometimes I'm in the mood, I'm gonna sleep in my pony's stall
Sometimes I'm in the mood, I ain't gonna do nothin' at all
Sometimes I'm in the mood, I wanna fly like a cannonball

## 宝贝，我在想你

有时候情绪来了，我想离开清冷的家
有时候情绪来了，我想听我的奶牛
　呻吟
有时候情绪来了，我想走上那高速路
可是还有，可是还有，我说哦，我说哦，我说
哦宝贝，我在想你

有时候情绪来了，主啊，我满得要溢出来
有时候情绪来了，我要立下我的遗嘱
有时候情绪来了，我要起身走上山岗
可是还有，可是还有，我说哦，我说哦，我说
哦宝贝，我在想你

有时候情绪来了，我想立马躺下死掉
有时候情绪来了，我想爬到天上去
有时候情绪来了，我要大笑直到哭泣
可是还有，我再说一次，我再说一次，我说
哦宝贝，我在想你

有时候情绪来了，我要睡我的小马厩
有时候情绪来了，我什么事都不想做
有时候情绪来了，我要像炮弹一样飞

But then again, but then again, I said oh, I said oh, I said

Oh babe, I'm in the mood for you

Sometimes I'm in the mood, I wanna back up against the wall

Sometimes I'm in the mood, I wanna run till I have to crawl

Sometimes I'm in the mood, I ain't gonna do nothin' at all

But then again, but then again, I said oh, I said oh, I said

Oh babe, I'm in the mood for you

Sometimes I'm in the mood, I wanna change my house around

Sometimes I'm in the mood, I'm gonna make a change in this
here town

Sometimes I'm in the mood, I'm gonna change the world
around

But then again, but then again, I said oh, I said oh, I said

Oh babe, I'm in the mood for you

可是还有，可是还有，我说哦，我说哦，我说
哦宝贝，我在想你

有时候情绪来了，我想后退靠在墙上
有时候情绪来了，我想奔跑直到在地上爬
有时候情绪来了，我什么事都不想做
可是还有，可是还有，我说哦，我说哦，我说
哦宝贝，我在想你

有时候情绪来了，我想把房子变个样
有时候情绪来了，我想改变这个
　小镇
有时候情绪来了，我想把世界
　变个样
可是还有，可是还有，我说哦，我说哦，我说
哦宝贝，我在想你

# LONG AGO, FAR AWAY

To preach of peace and brotherhood
Oh, what might be the cost!
A man he did it long ago
And they hung him on a cross
Long ago, far away
These things don't happen
No more, nowadays

The chains of slaves
They dragged the ground
With heads and hearts hung low
But it was during Lincoln's time
And it was long ago
Long ago, far away
Things like that don't happen
No more, nowadays

The war guns they went off wild
The whole world bled its blood
Men's bodies floated on the edge
Of oceans made of mud
Long ago, far away

## 很久以前，很远的地方

要宣扬和平与兄弟之爱
啊，可能付出什么代价！
一个人很久前这样做了
他们把他钉上了十字架
很久以前，很远的地方
这些事不会发生
如今，不会发生

奴隶们戴着镣铐
曳地而行
垂着头心情沉重
但那是在林肯时代
那是很久以前
很久以前，很远的地方
那样的事不会发生
如今，不会发生

战争中炮火纷飞
整个世界都在流血
人们的尸体漂浮在
泥浆的汪洋边缘
很久以前，很远的地方

Those kind of things don't happen
No more, nowadays

One man had much money
One man had not enough to eat
One man he lived just like a king
The other man begged on the street
Long ago, far away
Things like that don't happen
No more, nowadays

One man died of a knife so sharp
One man died from the bullet of a gun
One man died of a broken heart
To see the lynchin' of his son
Long ago, far away
Things like that don't happen
No more, nowadays

Gladiators killed themselves
It was during the Roman times
People cheered with bloodshot grins
As eyes and minds went blind
Long ago, far away
Things like that don't happen
No more, nowadays

那些事不会发生
如今，不会发生


一个人腰缠万贯
一个人吃不饱饭
一个人过得像国王
另一个人在街头讨钱
很久以前，很远的地方
那样的事不会发生
如今，不会发生


一个人死于这么尖的刀
一个人死于出自枪膛的子弹
一个人死于一颗破碎的心
他眼见着爱子因私刑毙命
很久以前，很远的地方
那样的事不会发生
如今，不会发生


角斗士自相残杀
那是在罗马时代
人们红眼血口地喝彩
眼睛和心都已失明
很久以前，很远的地方
那样的事不会发生
如今，不会发生

And to talk of peace and brotherhood

Oh, what might be the cost!

A man he did it long ago

And they hung him on a cross

Long ago, far away

Things like that don't happen

No more, nowadays, do they?

而要谈论和平与兄弟之爱
啊，可能付出什么代价！
一个人很久前这样做了
他们把他钉上了十字架
很久以前，很远的地方
那样的事不会发生
如今，不会发生，是吧？

## AIN'T GONNA GRIEVE

Well, I ain't a-gonna grieve no more, no more
Ain't a-gonna grieve no more, no more
Ain't a-gonna grieve no more, no more
And ain't a-gonna grieve no more

Come on brothers, join the band
Come on sisters, clap your hands
Tell everybody that's in the land
You ain't a-gonna grieve no more

Well, I ain't a-gonna grieve no more, no more
Ain't a-gonna grieve no more, no more
Ain't a-gonna grieve no more, no more
And ain't a-gonna grieve no more

Brown and blue and white and black
All one color on the one-way track
We got this far and ain't a-goin' back
And I ain't a-gonna grieve no more

## 不会哀悼 [1]

就这样，我不会再哀悼，不会了
不会再哀悼，不会了
不会再哀悼，不会了
我不会再哀悼

来吧弟兄们，加入这乐队
来吧姐妹们，双手拍起来
告诉这土地上的每个人
你不会再哀悼

就这样，我不会再哀悼，不会了
不会再哀悼，不会了
不会再哀悼，不会了
我不会再哀悼

棕色和蓝色和白色和黑色
在单行道上浑然一色
我们走这么远不会回头
并且我不会再哀悼

---

[1] 美国黑人圣歌中有《我主不会再哀悼》（"Ain't Gonna Grieve My Lord No More"）。

Well, I ain't a-gonna grieve no more, no more

Ain't a-gonna grieve no more, no more

Ain't a-gonna grieve no more, no more

I ain't a-gonna grieve no more

We're gonna notify your next of kin

You're gonna raise the roof until the house falls in

If you get knocked down get up again

We ain't a-gonna grieve no more

Well, I ain't a-gonna grieve no more, no more

Ain't a-gonna grieve no more, no more

Ain't a-gonna grieve no more, no more

I ain't a-gonna grieve no more

We'll sing this song all night long

Sing it to my baby from midnight on

She'll sing it to you when I'm dead and gone

Ain't a-gonna grieve no more

Well, I ain't a-gonna grieve no more, no more

Ain't a-gonna grieve no more, no more

Ain't a-gonna grieve no more, no more

I ain't a-gonna grieve no more

就这样，我不会再哀悼，不会了
不会再哀悼，不会了
不会再哀悼，不会了
我不会再哀悼

我们会通知你最近的亲属
你会吵翻屋顶直至把房子掀掉
如果你被击倒又再次立起
我们不会再哀悼

就这样，我不会再哀悼，不会了
不会再哀悼，不会了
不会再哀悼，不会了
我不会再哀悼

我们将整夜唱这首歌
从午夜开始唱给我的宝贝
我死后她会为你唱
不会再哀悼

就这样，我不会再哀悼，不会了
不会再哀悼，不会了
不会再哀悼，不会了
我不会再哀悼

# GYPSY LOU

If you getcha one girl, better get two

Case you run into Gypsy Lou

She's a ramblin' woman with a ramblin' mind

Always leavin' somebody behind

Hey, 'round the bend

Gypsy Lou's gone again

Gypsy Lou's gone again


Well, I seen the whole country through

Just to find Gypsy Lou

Seen it up, seen it down

Followin' Gypsy Lou around

Hey, 'round the bend

Gypsy Lou's gone again

Gypsy Lou's gone again


Well, I gotta stop and take some rest

My poor feet are second best

My poor feet are wearin' thin

Gypsy Lou's gone again

Hey, gone again

Gypsy Lou's 'round the bend

## 吉卜赛阿露

如果你要找女友，最好找俩
万一你碰上了吉卜赛阿露
她是个流浪女，有一颗流浪心
总是把男人甩了
嘿，在那转弯处
吉卜赛阿露又不见了
吉卜赛阿露又不见了

唉，我找遍了全国
就为了找到吉卜赛阿露
北上找，南下找
一路紧追着吉卜赛阿露
嘿，在那转弯处
吉卜赛阿露又不见了
吉卜赛阿露又不见了

唉，我得停下歇歇气
我可怜的脚不比从前
我可怜的脚越跑越细
吉卜赛阿露又不见了
嘿，又不见啦
吉卜赛阿露在转弯处

Gypsy Lou's 'round the bend

Well, seen her up in old Cheyenne
Turned my head and away she ran
From Denver Town to Wichita
Last I heard she's in Arkansas
Hey, 'round the bend
Gypsy Lou's gone again
Gypsy Lou's gone again

Well, I tell you what if you want to do
Tell you what, you'll wear out your shoes
If you want to wear out your shoes
Try and follow Gypsy Lou
Hey, gone again
Gypsy Lou's 'round the bend
Gypsy Lou's 'round the bend

Well, Gypsy Lou, I been told
Livin' down on Gallus Road
Gallus Road, Arlington
Moved away to Washington
Hey, 'round the bend
Gypsy Lou's gone again
Gypsy Lou's gone again

吉卜赛阿露在转弯处

唉，在老夏延市看到她了
我一转头，她又跑了
从丹佛镇到威奇托
上次听说她在阿肯色
嘿，在那转弯处
吉卜赛阿露又不见了
吉卜赛阿露又不见了

唉，要是你想找她会怎样
我告诉你，你的鞋子会踏破
如果你想把鞋子踏破
那就试试去追吉卜赛阿露
嘿，又不见啦
吉卜赛阿露在转弯处
吉卜赛阿露在转弯处

唉，吉卜赛阿露，有人告诉我
她住在加卢斯路
阿灵顿的加卢斯路
又搬去了华盛顿
嘿，在那转弯处
吉卜赛阿露又不见了
吉卜赛阿露又不见了

Well, I went down to Washington

Then she went to Oregon

I skipped the ground and hopped a train

She's back in Gallus Road again

Hey, I can't win

Gypsy Lou's gone again

Gypsy Lou's gone again


Well, the last I heard of Gypsy Lou

She's in a Memphis calaboose

She left one too many a boy behind

He committed suicide

Hey, you can't win

Gypsy Lou's gone again

Gypsy Lou's gone again

唉，我追到了华盛顿
她却去了俄勒冈
心急火燎我跳上火车
她又回了加卢斯路
嘿，我没法赢
吉卜赛阿露又不见了
吉卜赛阿露又不见了

唉，我最后听说吉卜赛阿露
她在孟菲斯蹲班房
她甩了那么多男孩
有一个自杀了
嘿，你没法赢
吉卜赛阿露又不见了
吉卜赛阿露又不见了

# LONG TIME GONE

My parents raised me tenderly
I was their only son
My mind got mixed with ramblin'
When I was all so young
And I left my home the first time
When I was twelve and one
I'm a long time a-comin', Maw
An' I'll be a long time gone

On the western side of Texas
On the Texas plains
I tried to find a job o' work
But they said I's young of age
My eyes they burned when I heard
"Go home where you belong!"
I'm a long time a-comin'
An' I'll be a long time gone

I remember when I's ramblin'
Around with the carnival trains
Different towns, different people
Somehow they're all the same

## 用很长时间走

我的父母小心将我养大
我是他们唯一的儿子
却满脑子出去闯荡的想法
当我还是个小孩子
我就第一次离开家
当时我十三岁
我用很长时间来，妈妈
我也会用很长时间走

在得克萨斯西部
在得克萨斯平原
我试着去找工作
可他们说我年纪还小
我眼睛冒火当我听到
"哪儿来的回哪儿去！"
我用很长时间来
我也会用很长时间走

记得我一路漂泊
搭乘着狂欢节列车
不同城镇，不同的人
不知为什么他们又都是一样的

I remember children's faces best
I remember travelin' on
I'm a long time a-comin'
I'll be a long time gone

I once loved a fair young maid
An' I ain't too big to tell
If she broke my heart a single time
She broke it ten or twelve
I walked and talked all by myself
I did not tell no one
I'm a long time a-comin', babe
An' I'll be a long time gone

Many times by the highwayside
I tried to flag a ride
With bloodshot eyes and gritting teeth
I'd watch the cars roll by
The empty air hung in my head
I's thinkin' all day long
I'm a long time a-comin'
I'll be a long time gone

You might see me on your crossroads
When I'm a-passin' through
Remember me how you wished to

记忆最深的是孩子们的脸
我记得一直在路上
我用很长时间来
我也会用很长时间走


我爱过一个美丽的小女孩
而我也还不大，没法说出来
假如她伤我心一次
她便伤了它十次十二次
我一个人走路和说话
这事儿没告诉任何人
我用很长时间来，宝贝
我也会用很长时间走


许多次在公路边
我做出手势想搭便车
紧咬着牙眼睛充血
看着车子滚滚驶过
我的脑中空空荡荡
整天想的都是
我用很长时间来
我也会用很长时间走


在十字路口你可能见过我
当时的我正好路过
用你喜欢的方式记忆吧

As I'm a-driftin' from your view
I ain't got the time to think about it
I got too much to get done
Well, I'm a long time comin'
An' I'll be a long time gone

If I can't help somebody
With a word or song
If I can't show somebody
They are travelin' wrong
But I know I ain't no prophet
An' I ain't no prophet's son
I'm just a long time a-comin'
An' I'll be a long time gone

So you can have your beauty
It's skin deep and it only lies
And you can have your youth
It'll rot before your eyes
Just give to me my gravestone
With it clearly carved upon:
"I's a long time a-comin'
An' I'll be a long time gone"

当我飘出你的视野
我没有时间去多想
我有太多事要做
哦，我用很长时间来
我也会用很长时间走

如果我不能帮到别人
以一句话或一首歌
如果我不能向人指明
他们的路走错了
我知道我不是先知
我也不是先知的儿子
只是我用很长时间来
我也会用很长时间走

所以你可以有你的美
它很肤浅它只会欺骗
你也可以有你的青春
它将会腐烂在你眼前
就给我一块墓碑吧
上面清楚地刻下：
"我用很长时间来
我也会用很长时间走"

## WALKIN' DOWN THE LINE

Well, I'm walkin' down the line
I'm walkin' down the line
An' I'm walkin' down the line
My feet'll be a-flyin'
To tell about my troubled mind

I got a heavy-headed gal
I got a heavy-headed gal
I got a heavy-headed gal
She ain't a-feelin' well
When she's better only time will tell

Well, I'm walkin' down the line
I'm walkin' down the line
An' I'm walkin' down the line
My feet'll be a-flyin'
To tell about my troubled mind

My money comes and goes
My money comes and goes
My money comes and goes
And rolls and flows and rolls and flows

## 沿路走下去

嗯，我在沿路走下去
我在沿路走下去
而我沿路走下去
我的脚就会飞起
说出我烦恼的心事

我有一个头昏昏的女友
我有一个头昏昏的女友
我有一个头昏昏的女友
她感觉不太好
何时会好只有时间知道

嗯，我在沿路走下去
我在沿路走下去
而我沿路走下去
我的脚就会飞起
说出我烦恼的心事

我的钱来了又去
我的钱来了又去
我的钱来了又去
滚过来又流走，滚过来又流走

Through the holes in the pockets in my clothes

Well, I'm walkin' down the line
I'm walkin' down the line
An' I'm walkin' down the line
My feet'll be a-flyin'
To tell about my troubled mind

I see the morning light
I see the morning light
Well, it's not because
I'm an early riser
I didn't go to sleep last night

Well, I'm walkin' down the line
I'm walkin' down the line
An' I'm walkin' down the line
My feet'll be a-flyin'
To tell about my troubled mind

I got my walkin' shoes
I got my walkin' shoes
I got my walkin' shoes
An' I ain't a-gonna lose
I believe I got the walkin' blues

穿过我衣服口袋的漏洞

嗯，我在沿路走下去
我在沿路走下去
而我沿路走下去
我的脚就会飞起
说出我烦恼的心事

我看见了曙光
我看见了曙光
嗯，不是因为
我起得早
昨夜我一宿没睡

嗯，我在沿路走下去
我在沿路走下去
而我沿路走下去
我的脚就会飞起
说出我烦恼的心事

我有我的行路鞋
我有我的行路鞋
我有我的行路鞋
所以我不会输掉
我确信我有行路蓝调

Well, I'm walkin' down the line

I'm walkin' down the line

An' I'm walkin' down the line

My feet'll be a-flyin'

To tell about my troubled mind

嗯，我在沿路走下去
我在沿路走下去
而我沿路走下去
我的脚就会飞起
说出我烦恼的心事

# TRAIN A-TRAVELIN'

There's an iron train a-travelin' that's been a-rollin' through the
   years
With a firebox of hatred and a furnace full of fears
If you ever heard its sound or seen its blood-red broken frame
Then you heard my voice a-singin' and you know my name

Did you ever stop to wonder 'bout the hatred that it holds?
Did you ever see its passengers, its crazy mixed-up souls?
Did you ever start a-thinkin' that you gotta stop that train?
Then you heard my voice a-singin' and you know my name

Do you ever get tired of the preachin' sounds of fear
When they're hammered at your head and pounded in your
   ear?
Have you ever asked about it and not been answered plain?
Then you heard my voice a-singin' and you know my name

I'm a-wonderin' if the leaders of the nations understand
This murder-minded world that they're leavin' in my hands
Have you ever laid awake at night and wondered 'bout the
   same?
Then you've heard my voice a-singin' and you know my name

## 旅行火车

有一列钢铁的旅行火车驶过了
　许多年
它的炉膛里是仇恨，锅炉里充满恐惧
如果你听见过它的声音看见过它血红的破架子
那么你就听见我的歌声知道我的名字

你可曾停下来想过它包藏了什么仇恨？
你可曾见过它的乘客，它疯狂混乱的灵魂？
你可曾动过念你必须停下这列火车？
那么你就听见我的歌声知道我的名字

你是否厌倦了那出自恐惧的宣讲声
当它锤打着你的头撞击着你的
　耳鼓？
你可曾问过这些却得不到明确回应？
那么你就听见我的歌声知道我的名字

我想知道各国的领导人是否理解
他们交在我手上的这杀机重重的世界
整夜无眠时你可曾有过同样的
　困惑？
那么你就听到了我的歌声知道我的名字

Have you ever had it on your lips or said it in your head

That the person standin' next to you just might be misled?

Does the raving of the maniacs make your insides go insane?

Then you've heard my voice a-singin' and you know my name

Do the kill-crazy bandits and the haters get you down?

Does the preachin' and the politics spin your head around?

Does the burning of the buses give your heart a pain?

Then you've heard my voice a-singin' and you know my name

你可曾嘴上这么说或心里这么念叨
站你旁边的那人可能已被误导？
那些疯子的胡话是否让你精神错乱？
那么你就听到了我的歌声知道我的名字

嗜血的亡命徒和厌世者让你沉重吗？
布道和政治让你晕头转向吗？
公交车的燃烧让你心痛吗？
那么你就听到了我的歌声知道我的名字

# BALLAD OF DONALD WHITE

My name is Donald White, you see
I stand before you all
I was judged by you a murderer
And the hangman's knot must fall
I will die upon the gallows pole
When the moon is shining clear
And these are my final words
That you will ever hear

I left my home in Kansas
When I was very young
I landed in the old Northwest
Seattle, Washington
Although I'd a-traveled many miles
I never made a friend
For I could never get along in life
With people that I met

If I had some education
To give me a decent start
I might have been a doctor or
A master in the arts

## 唐纳德·怀特之歌

我名叫唐纳德·怀特，瞧
我站在你们所有人面前
被你们指控为杀人犯
刽子手的绳索终将落下
我会死在绞架上
当着那明月高悬
下面将是你们听到的
我最后的遗言

在我年纪还很小时
我就离开了家乡堪萨斯
落脚在老西北
华盛顿州的西雅图
虽然我走了很长的路
却从没交上朋友
因为我遇到的人
我都无法跟他们在生活中相处

如果我受过一些教育
给我一个体面的开始
我可能成为医生或者
艺术界的才子

But I used my hands for stealing
When I was very young
And they locked me down in jailhouse cells
That's how my life begun

Oh, the inmates and the prisoners
I found they were my kind
And it was there inside the bars
I found my peace of mind
But the jails they were too crowded
Institutions overflowed
So they turned me loose to walk upon
Life's hurried tangled road

And there's danger on the ocean
Where the salt sea waves split high
And there's danger on the battlefield
Where the shells of bullets fly
And there's danger in this open world
Where men strive to be free
And for me the greatest danger
Was in society

So I asked them to send me back
To the institution home
But they said they were too crowded

但是我用两手偷
在我年纪还很小时
于是他们把我关进牢房
我的生活由此开启

哦，犯人和囚徒
我发现他们与我是同类
而在铁栏后面
我找到了内心的平静
但是监狱太挤了
收容所人多得漫出来
所以他们放我出来
走上人生这匆匆缠缠的路

而危险在海上
是咸海浪高高炸碎
而危险在战场
是子弹纷飞
而危险在这开放世界
是人人为自由奋争
而对我来说最大的危险
是身处社会中

所以我求他们把我送回去
送回收容所的家
但他们说那地方太挤

For me they had no room
I got down on my knees and begged
"Oh, please put me away"
But they would not listen to my plea
Or nothing I would say

And so it was on Christmas Eve
In the year of '59
It was on that night I killed a man
I did not try to hide
The jury found me guilty
And I won't disagree
For I knew that it would happen
If I wasn't put away

And I'm glad I've had no parents
To care for me or cry
For now they will never know
The horrible death I die
And I'm also glad I've had no friends
To see me in disgrace
For they'll never see that hangman's hood
Wrap around my face

Farewell unto the old north woods
Of which I used to roam

腾不出空间给我
我跪下来求啊
"啊，行行好把我带走吧"
但他们不为所动
无论我怎样磨破嘴皮

于是在一九五九年
平安夜
夜里我杀了人
我没打算躲
陪审团认定我有罪
我也没异议
因为我知道它迟早发生
如果不把我关进监狱

而我庆幸我无父无母
用不着关心我为我哭泣
他们永远都不会知晓
我死得有多恐怖
我也庆幸我没有朋友
会看到我如此不堪
他们永远不会看到刽子手
将头套罩在我脸上

永别了北方老林
我一度流连的地方

Farewell unto the crowded bars

Of which've been my home

Farewell to all you people

Who think the worst of me

I guess you'll feel much better when

I'm on that hanging tree

But there's just one question

Before they kill me dead

I'm wondering just how much

To you I really said

Concerning all the boys that come

Down a road like me

Are they enemies or victims

Of your society?

永别了人挤人的酒吧
你们一度是我的家
永别了各位
你们只念着我的坏
我想这回你们感觉好多了
当我吊死在那棵树上

但是还有一个问题
在他们处死我之前
我想知道你们
听清了多少我说的话
关于所有那些
走上我这条路的孩子
他们是你们这社会的敌人
还是受害者？

# QUIT YOUR LOW DOWN WAYS

Oh, you can read out your Bible
You can fall down on your knees, pretty mama
And pray to the Lord
But it ain't gonna do no good

You're gonna need
You're gonna need my help someday
Well, if you can't quit your sinnin'
Please quit your low down ways

Well, you can run down to the White House
You can gaze at the Capitol Dome, pretty mama
You can pound on the President's gate
But you oughta know by now it's gonna be too late

You're gonna need
You're gonna need my help someday
Well, if you can't quit your sinnin'
Please quit your low down ways

## 戒掉你的低劣行径

哦，你可以朗读你的《圣经》
可以跪倒在地，漂亮妈妈 [1]
然后向天主祷告
但是这些都没用

你会需要
有一天你会需要我帮助
好吧，如果你不能戒掉你的罪过
那么请戒掉你的低劣行径

好，你可以跑白宫去
可以凝望国会大厦的圆顶，漂亮妈妈
你可以去敲总统的门
但你该知道现在为时已晚

你会需要
有一天你会需要我帮助
好吧，如果你不能戒掉你的罪过
那么请戒掉你的低劣行径

---

[1] 这里的"妈妈"，是俚语中对情人的称呼。

Well, you can run down to the desert

Throw yourself on the burning sand

You can raise up your right hand, pretty mama

But you better understand you done lost your one good man


You're gonna need

You're gonna need my help someday

Well, if you can't quit your sinnin'

Please quit your low down ways


And you can hitchhike on the highway

You can stand all alone by the side of the road

You can try to flag a ride back home, pretty mama

But you can't ride in my car no more


You're gonna need

You're gonna need my help someday

Well, if you can't quit your sinnin'

Please quit your low down ways


Oh, you can read out your Bible

You can fall down on your knees, pretty mama

And pray to the Lord

But it ain't gonna do no good


You're gonna need

好，你可以跑到沙漠去
把自己扔在燃烧的沙子上
你可以举起你的右手，漂亮妈妈
但是你最好明白你刚失去一个好男人

你会需要
有一天你会需要我帮助
好吧，如果你不能戒掉你的罪过
那么请戒掉你的低劣行径

你还可以去公路上搭便车
可以独自站在路边
可以招辆车子回家，漂亮妈妈
但是你不能再坐我的车了

你会需要
有一天你会需要我帮助
好吧，如果你不能戒掉你的罪过
那么请戒掉你的低劣行径

哦，你可以朗读你的《圣经》
可以跪倒在地，漂亮妈妈
然后向天主祷告
但是这些都没用

你会需要

You're gonna need my help someday

Well, if you can't quit your sinnin'

Please quit your low down ways

有一天你会需要我帮助
好吧，如果你不能戒掉你的罪过
那么请戒掉你的低劣行径

# I'D HATE TO BE YOU ON THAT DREADFUL DAY

Well, your clock is gonna stop
At Saint Peter's gate
Ya gonna ask him what time it is
He's gonna say, "It's too late"
Hey, hey!
I'd sure hate to be you
On that dreadful day

You're gonna start to sweat
And you ain't gonna stop
You're gonna have a nightmare
And never wake up
Hey, hey, hey!
I'd sure hate to be you
On that dreadful day

You're gonna cry for pills
And your head's gonna be in a knot
But the pills are gonna cost more
Than what you've got
Hey, hey!
I'd sure hate to be you

## 我真不想在那个可怕的日子成为你

唉，你的钟会停摆
在圣彼得的门前
你会问他几点了
他会说："太晚了"
嘿，嘿！
我真不想成为你
在那个可怕的日子

你会开始冒汗
并且止不住
你会做一个噩梦
并且永不会醒
嘿，嘿，嘿！
我真不想成为你
在那个可怕的日子

你会哭着求药
而且你的脑袋会打结
但是药太贵了
超过了你拥有的
嘿，嘿！
我真不想成为你

On that dreadful day

You're gonna have to walk naked
Can't ride in no car
You're gonna let ev'rybody see
Just what you are
Hey, hey!
I'd sure hate to be you
On that dreadful day

Well, the good wine's a-flowin'
For five cents a quart
You're gonna look in your moneybags
And find you're one cent short
Hey, hey, hey!
I'd sure hate to be you
On that dreadful day

You're gonna yell and scream
"Don't anybody care?"
You're gonna hear out a voice say
"Shoulda listened when you heard the word down there"
Hey, hey!
I'd sure hate to be you
On that dreadful day

在那个可怕的日子

你必须赤身裸体地走
不会有车子坐
让所有人都看到
你就是这个样子
嘿，嘿！
我真不想成为你
在那个可怕的日子

唉，美酒到处流
一夸脱五分钱
你会翻遍你的钱包
发现差了一分钱
嘿，嘿，嘿！
我真不想成为你
在那个可怕的日子

你会大喊大叫
"没有人在乎吗？"
你会听到一个声音说
"当时听见这话时你该听听"
嘿，嘿！
我真不想成为你
在那个可怕的日子

## MIXED UP CONFUSION

I got mixed up confusion
Man, it's a-killin' me
Well, there's too many people
And they're all too hard to please

Well, my hat's in my hand
Babe, I'm walkin' down the line
An' I'm lookin' for a woman
Whose head's mixed up like mine

Well, my head's full of questions
My temp'rature's risin' fast
Well, I'm lookin' for some answers
But I don't know who to ask

But I'm walkin' and wonderin'
And my poor feet don't ever stop
Seein' my reflection
I'm hung over, hung down, hung up!

## 纠结的困惑

我陷入纠结的困惑
老弟，我要死了
唉，太多人
而且他们都难以取悦

好吧，帽子拿手里
宝贝，我沿这条路走下去
我在找一个女人
她的脑子跟我一样纠结

唉，我满脑子是问题
体温飙升
唉，我在找答案
但是不知道能问谁

但是我边走边想
可怜的脚不曾停歇
我看见自己的样子
迷迷糊糊，低着头，念念不忘！

# HERO BLUES

Yes, the gal I got
I swear she's the screaming end
She wants me to be a hero
So she can tell all her friends

Well, she begged, she cried
She pleaded with me all last night
Well, she begged, she cried
She pleaded with me all last night
She wants me to go out
And find somebody to fight

She reads too many books
She got new movies inside her head
She reads too many books
She got movies inside her head
She wants me to walk out running
She wants me to crawl back dead

You need a different kinda man, babe
One that can grab and hold your heart
Need a different kind of man, babe

## 英雄蓝调

是啊，我找的这女人
我发誓她是个极品
她要我做英雄
她好向朋友们炫耀

唉，她哀求，她哭号
昨天一整夜都在求我
唉，她哀求，她哭号
昨天一整夜都在求我
她要我到外面去
去找人干仗

她读了太多书
脑瓜里都是新电影
她读了太多书
脑瓜里都是电影
她要我出门跑
她要我爬着回来死掉

你要的是与众不同的男人，宝贝
一个能抓住并握紧你的心的
你要的是与众不同的男人，宝贝

One that can hold and grab your heart

You need a different kind of man, babe

You need Napoleon Boneeparte

Well, when I'm dead

No more good times will I crave

When I'm dead

No more good times will I crave

You can stand and shout hero

All over my lonesome grave

一个能抓住并握紧你的心的
你要的是与众不同的男人，宝贝
你要的是拿破仑·波泥巴 [1]

好吧，等我死了
我不再渴望好时光
等我死了
我不再渴望好时光
你可以站上去大喊英雄
在我寂寞的坟头

---

[1] 把"拿破仑·波拿巴"有意写作"拿破仑·波泥巴"，表示调侃。

# TOMORROW IS A LONG TIME

If today was not an endless highway
If tonight was not a crooked trail
If tomorrow wasn't such a long time
Then lonesome would mean nothing to you at all
Yes, and only if my own true love was waitin'
Yes, and if I could hear her heart a-softly poundin'
Only if she was lyin' by me
Then I'd lie in my bed once again

I can't see my reflection in the waters
I can't speak the sounds that show no pain
I can't hear the echo of my footsteps
Or can't remember the sound of my own name
Yes, and only if my own true love was waitin'
Yes, and if I could hear her heart a-softly poundin'
Only if she was lyin' by me
Then I'd lie in my bed once again

There's beauty in the silver, singin' river
There's beauty in the sunrise in the sky
But none of these and nothing else can touch the beauty
That I remember in my true love's eyes

## 明天是一段漫长的时光

如若今天不是一条无尽的长路
如若今晚不是一条蜿蜒的小径
如若明天不是一段如此漫长的时光
那么，寂寞于你也就毫无意义
是的，只有当我的真爱在等待
是的，而且我能听见她的心在温柔跳荡
只有她睡在我身旁
我才会再次躺到我的床上

我看不见水中我的倒影
我发不出不带痛苦的声音
我听不到我脚步的回响
也记不得自己的名字如何发音
是的，只有当我的真爱在等待
是的，而且我能听见她的心在温柔跳荡
只有她睡在我身旁
我才会再次躺到我的床上

银色的吟唱的河流里有美
天空中的日出里有美
但这些和其他的一切
都不及我记忆中真爱眼睛里的美

Yes, and only if my own true love was waitin'

Yes, and if I could hear her heart a-softly poundin'

Only if she was lyin' by me

Then I'd lie in my bed once again

是的，只有当我的真爱在等待
是的，而且我能听见她的心在温柔跳荡
只有她睡在我身旁
我才会再次躺到我的床上

# BOB DYLAN'S NEW ORLEANS RAG

I was sittin' on a stump
Down in New Orleans
I was feelin' kinda low down
Dirty and mean
Along came a fella
And he didn't even ask
He says, "I know of a woman
That can fix you up fast"
I didn't think twice
I said like I should
"Let's go find this lady
That can do me some good"
We walked across the river
On a sailin' spree
And we came to a door
Called one-oh-three

I was just about ready
To give it a little knock
When out comes a fella

## 鲍勃·迪伦的新奥尔良拉格 [1]

我坐在木桩上
在南方的新奥尔良
心情有点儿低落
龌龊而阴沉
旁边来了个伙计
问都不问一声
就说，"我认识个女的
能快速解决你的问题"
我想都没想
理所当然地应道
"我们去找这位女士
她会对我有好处"
屁颠颠坐着船
我们过了河
来到一扇门前
门牌一〇三

我正要抬手
轻轻敲门
里面出来一个伙计

---

[1] 拉格，拉格泰姆的简称，一种爵士乐体裁。

Who couldn't even walk

He's linkin' and a-slinkin'

Couldn't stand on his feet

And he moaned and he groaned

And he shuffled down the street

Well, out of the door

There comes another man

He wiggled and he wobbled

He couldn't hardly stand

He had this frightened

Look in his eyes

Like he just fought a bear

He was ready to die

Well, I peeked through the key crack

Comin' down the hall

Was a long-legged man

Who couldn't hardly crawl

He muttered and he uttered

In broken French

And he looked like he'd been through

A monkey wrench

Well, by this time

I was a-scared to knock

I was a-scared to move

连走路都不行了
两腿打着绊，跌跌撞撞
站都站不稳
边哀叹边呻吟
拖着脚走到街上
哦，门里又出来了
另一个男人
边扭边摇晃
几乎站立不住
两只眼睛里
有那么一种害怕
像是刚跟熊打了架
准备这就一命归西

哦，我透过钥匙孔望
看见走廊里移过来
一个长腿男人
几乎都不能爬
嘴巴里嘟嘟囔囔
说着一堆烂法语
那样子就像是
他刚被活动扳手修理过

哦，到了这个时候
我吓得啊不敢敲门
吓得啊不敢动

I's in a state of shock

I hummed a little tune

And I shuffled my feet

And I started walkin' backwards

Down that broad street

Well, I got to the corner

I tried my best to smile

I turned around the corner

And I ran a bloody mile

Man, I wasn't runnin'

'Cause I was sick

I was just a-runnin'

To get out of there quick

Well, I tripped right along

And I'm a-wheezin' in my chest

I musta run a mile

In a minute or less

I walked on a log

And I tripped on a stump

I caught a fast freight

With a one-arm jump

So, if you're travelin' down

Louisiana way

And you feel kinda lonesome

And you need a place to stay

处于休克状态
我嘴里哼着小调
然后拖着脚
然后开始倒行
倒退到大马路上
哦，我到了街角
强作微笑
我转过了街角
然后跑了该死的一英里
老兄，我这样跑
并非因为我有毛病
我这样跑
只是要快点离开那里

哦，我一路踉跄
呼哧呼哧直喘
我得跑它个一英里
在一分钟内或更短
我踩到了一块木头
又绊到一截木桩
追上了一列货车
一只手抓住跳上去
所以，如果你在旅行
南下到路易斯安那
并且觉得有点儿寂寞
想找个地方歇歇

Man, you're better off

In your misery

Than to tackle that lady

At one-oh-three

老兄啊，你最好待在

自己的凄惨里

也胜过去对付那位

住一〇三的女士

## ALL OVER YOU

Well, if I had to do it all over again
Babe, I'd do it all over you
And if I had to wait for ten thousand years
Babe, I'd even do that too
Well, a dog's got his bone in the alley
A cat, she's got nine lives
A millionaire's got a million dollars
King Saud's got four hundred wives
Well, ev'rybody's got somethin'
That they're lookin' forward to
I'm lookin' forward to when I can do it all again
And babe, I'll do it all over you

Well, if I had my way tomorrow or today
Babe, I'd run circles all around
I'd jump up in the wind, do a somersault and spin
I'd even dance a jig on the ground
Well, everybody gets their hour
Everybody gets their time
Little David when he picked up his pebbles
Even Sampson after he went blind
Well, everybody gets the chance

## 全是因为你

好吧，如果我不得不重来一遍
宝贝，全是因为你我才这么做
如果我不得不再等一万年
宝贝，就算这样我也情愿
好吧，一条狗在胡同里弄到了骨头
一只猫，她有九条命
百万富翁有一百万美元
沙特国王有四百佳丽
好吧，人人都有
他所期盼的东西
我期盼的是我能重来一遍
宝贝，我做这些全是因为你

好吧，如果明天或今天我说了算
宝贝，我会绕圈狂奔
我会跳进风中，翻个筋斗然后旋转
甚至在地上跳段吉格舞
好吧，人人都有属于自己的时刻
人人都有属于自己的时辰
少年大卫捡起石头之际
甚至参孙双目失明之后
好吧，人人都有机会

To do what they want to do

When my time arrives you better run for your life

'Cause babe, I'll do it all over you


Well, I don't need no money, I just need a day that's sunny

Baby, and my days are gonna come

And I grab me a pint, you know that I'm a giant

When you hear me yellin', "Fee-fi-fo-fum"

Well, you cut me like a jigsaw puzzle

You made me to a walkin' wreck

Then you pushed my heart through my backbone

Then you knocked off my head from my neck

Well, if I'm ever standin' steady

A-doin' what I want to do

Well, I tell you little lover that you better run for cover

'Cause babe, I'll do it all over you


I'm just restin' at your gate so that I won't be late

And, momma, I'm a-just sittin' on the shelf

Look out your window fair and you'll see me squattin' there

Just a-fumblin' and a-mumblin' to myself

Well, after my cigarette's been smoked up

After all my liquor's been drunk

After my dreams are dreamed out

After all my thoughts have been thunk

Well, after I do some of these things

做他想做的事
当我的时辰到来你最好快逃命
因为宝贝，我做这些全是因为你

好吧，我不需要钱，我只要一个艳阳天
宝贝，而我的日子就要来了
我猛灌下一品脱酒，你知道我是巨人
这时你听到我大叫："噫—吁—嘻—喂"
好吧，你把我剪得像一幅拼图
你让我成了行尸走肉
然后你从我的脊柱挤出我的心
然后你从脖子上打落我的头
好吧，一旦我站稳了
做我想做的事
好吧，我告诉你小爱人你最好快躲
因为宝贝，我做这些全是因为你

我就歇在你门边这样不会迟到
而且，妈妈，我就坐在那架子上
你只要往窗外一望就会看到我缩在那里
净在摸摸索索叽叽咕咕自言自语
好吧，等我的烟抽完了
等我的酒喝完了
等我的梦做完了
等我的事想完了
好吧，等这些事都办了

I'm gonna do what I have to do

And I tell you on the side, that you better run and hide

'Cause babe, I'll do it all over you

我就会做我必须做的

对了顺便告诉你，你最好快跑快藏好

因为宝贝，我做这些全是因为你

# JOHN BROWN

John Brown went off to war to fight on a foreign shore
His mama sure was proud of him!
He stood straight and tall in his uniform and all
His mama's face broke out all in a grin

"Oh son, you look so fine, I'm glad you're a son of mine
You make me proud to know you hold a gun
Do what the captain says, lots of medals you will get
And we'll put them on the wall when you come home"

As that old train pulled out, John's ma began to shout
Tellin' ev'ryone in the neighborhood:
"That's my son that's about to go, he's a soldier now, you know"
She made well sure her neighbors understood

She got a letter once in a while and her face broke into a smile
As she showed them to the people from next door
And she bragged about her son with his uniform and gun
And these things you called a good old-fashioned war

Oh! Good old-fashioned war!

## 约翰·布朗

约翰·布朗参军到大洋彼岸打仗
他的妈妈真为他骄傲!
他穿着军装挺拔又高大
妈妈的脸上乐开了花

"啊儿子,你真帅,妈妈真是高兴
知道你要握起枪,让我好自豪
你要听长官的话,你会得很多勋章
等你回家咱们把它挂在墙上"

旧火车缓缓驶出,约翰的妈妈开始喊
告诉附近每个人:
"那是我儿子要走了,他是个军人,你们知道吧"
她要让她的邻居们都确确实实晓得

每隔一阵子她就收到信,让她一脸欢喜
她把信拿给隔壁邻居
她吹她的儿子,吹他的制服和枪
还有这些你们称为老派战争的东西

啊! 老派战争!

Then the letters ceased to come, for a long time they did not
   come
They ceased to come for about ten months or more
Then a letter finally came saying, "Go down and meet the train
Your son's a-coming home from the war"

She smiled and went right down, she looked everywhere
   around
But she could not see her soldier son in sight
But as all the people passed, she saw her son at last
When she did she could hardly believe her eyes

Oh his face was all shot up and his hand was all blown off
And he wore a metal brace around his waist
He whispered kind of slow, in a voice she did not know
While she couldn't even recognize his face!

Oh! Lord! Not even recognize his face

"Oh tell me, my darling son, pray tell me what they done
How is it you come to be this way?"
He tried his best to talk but his mouth could hardly move
And the mother had to turn her face away

"Don't you remember, Ma, when I went off to war
You thought it was the best thing I could do?

然后信不再来，很久都没
　一封
至少十个月没有音讯
然后终于来了一封，上面写："去车站接车
你儿子从战场回来了"

她微笑着即刻去车站，在那里四下
　张望
但是看不到她的军人儿子
等所有人都走过去，她终于看到了儿子
这时她简直不相信自己的眼睛

啊他的脸上都是疤一只手整个没了
腰间戴着一圈金属支架
他那么慢低声说话，她听不出是他的声音
甚至她连他的脸都认不出来了！

啊！主啊！他的脸都认不出来了！

"啊告诉我，亲爱的儿子，求你告诉我发生了什么
你怎么会变成这个样子？"
他极力地想回答，但嘴巴几乎动不了
于是母亲只好别过脸去

"你不记得了，妈，当初我出去打仗
你认为那是我能做的最好的事？

I was on the battleground, you were home . . . acting proud
You wasn't there standing in my shoes"


"Oh, and I thought when I was there, God, what am I doing
   here?
I'm a-tryin' to kill somebody or die tryin'
But the thing that scared me most was when my enemy came
   close
And I saw that his face looked just like mine"


Oh! Lord! Just like mine!


"And I couldn't help but think, through the thunder rolling and
   stink
That I was just a puppet in a play
And through the roar and smoke, this string is finally broke
And a cannonball blew my eyes away"


As he turned away to walk, his Ma was still in shock
At seein' the metal brace that helped him stand
But as he turned to go, he called his mother close
And he dropped his medals down into her hand

我在战场，你在家……表现骄傲
你从没体会过我的境况"

"啊，到了那里我想，上帝，我在这儿
　　干什么？
我奋力杀人或者奋力死
但让我最害怕的是敌人
　　靠近时
我看到他的脸和我的一样"

啊！主啊！和我的一样！

"而我不禁想到，穿过那枪炮雷鸣和
　　恶臭的我
不过是戏里的傀儡
而经过战火呼啸和硝烟弥漫，这条弦终于断了
一颗炮弹炸瞎了我的眼"

他说着转过身挪步，他的妈妈还在震惊
茫然地看着帮助他站立的金属支架
而当他转身要离开，他喊他的母亲走近
将他的勋章丢进了她的手心

## FAREWELL

Oh it's fare thee well my darlin' true
I'm leavin' in the first hour of the morn
I'm bound off for the bay of Mexico
Or maybe the coast of Californ
So it's fare thee well my own true love
We'll meet another day, another time
It ain't the leavin'
That's a-grievin' me
But my true love who's bound to stay behind

Oh the weather is against me and the wind blows hard
And the rain she's a-turnin' into hail
I still might strike it lucky on a highway goin' west
Though I'm travelin' on a path beaten trail
So it's fare thee well my own true love
We'll meet another day, another time
It ain't the leavin'
That's a-grievin' me
But my true love who's bound to stay behind

I will write you a letter from time to time
As I'm ramblin' you can travel with me too

## 告别

啊珍重，我忠实的爱人
我就要离去，在黎明的第一个时辰
我将动身去墨西哥湾
或者也许去加利福尼亚海滨
所以请珍重，我忠实的爱人
某年某日我们还会相会
并不是离别
让我伤悲
而是我忠实的爱人必定要留下

啊天气跟我作对风刮得好大
而雨它变成了冰雹
西行路上我仍可能走运搭上便车
虽然我走在一条人迹罕至的小道
所以请珍重，我忠实的爱人
某年某日我们还会相会
并不是离别
让我伤悲
而是我忠实的爱人必定要留下

我会不时给你写信
就仿佛你也和我一起旅行

With my head, my heart and my hands, my love
I will send what I learn back home to you
So it's fare thee well my own true love
We'll meet another day, another time
It ain't the leavin'
That's a-grievin' me
But my true love who's bound to stay behind

I will tell you of the laughter and of troubles
Be them somebody else's or my own
With my hands in my pockets and my coat collar high
I will travel unnoticed and unknown
So it's fare thee well my own true love
We'll meet another day, another time
It ain't the leavin'
That's a-grievin' me
But my true love who's bound to stay behind

I've heard tell of a town where I might as well be bound
It's down around the old Mexican plains
They say that the people are all friendly there
And all they ask of you is your name
So it's fare thee well my own true love
We'll meet another day, another time
It ain't the leavin'

和我的头、我的心、我的手，我的爱
我将把我学到的也给你寄回家
所以请珍重，我忠实的爱人
某年某日我们还会相会
并不是离别
让我伤悲
而是我忠实的爱人必定要留下

我会告诉你欢笑告诉你烦恼
不管那是别人的还是属于我自己
手插进口袋衣领高高竖起
这将是无人注意无人知晓的旅程
所以请珍重，我忠实的爱人
某年某日我们还会相会
并不是离别
让我伤悲
而是我忠实的爱人必定要留下

那个小镇的传闻我听说过我也或将前往
它坐落在老墨西哥平原一带
他们说那儿的人都很友善
除了问你的名字其他一概不管
所以请珍重，我忠实的爱人
某年某日我们还会相会
并不是离别

That's a-grievin' me

But my true love who's bound to stay behind

让我伤悲
而是我忠实的爱人必定要留下

# THE FREEWHEELIN' BOB DYLAN
## 自由不羁的鲍勃·迪伦

答案在风中飘

北国姑娘

战争大师

在公路上走着

鲍勃·迪伦的蓝调

暴雨将至

别多想了，没事了

鲍勃·迪伦的梦

牛津城

科琳娜，科琳娜

亲爱的，只求你再给我一次机会

我将会自由

附加歌词

你要怎么做　　　　　　　　　七重诅咒

红翼之墙　　　　　　　　　　尘土飞扬的老露天游乐场

谁杀了戴维·摩尔

① I found a piano job & started to play
Bloking my lungs out for dollar day
Blowed inside out and upside down
Boss said he liked my sound
Dollar a days worth

② ~~I finally~~
~~That I got me a piano bar place~~
~~I worked and for a few an hour~~
~~...~~
~~...~~ After weeks of me hanging around
I got a job in this man's town
In a ~~little~~ place ~~with~~ gray
My name was even posted on the ~~door~~ outside of the place

③ Now a very great man once said
That some people rob you with a fountain pen
It ~~just~~ didn't take you long to find out
Just what he was talking about
That — table — forks — knives — cut something

④ So one mornin when the sun was warm
I ~~...~~ this here town
I pulled my cap down over my eyes
Headed out for western skies
Goodbye N.Y. Howdy East Orange

《自由不羁的鲍勃·迪伦》是迪伦第 2 张录音室专辑，由哥伦比亚唱片公司于 1963 年 5 月 27 日发行。这张专辑首次展示了迪伦高度个人化的民谣创作，即在英语传统歌曲旋律中，塞入深受《圣经》、民歌、法国象征主义和"垮掉的一代"作家影响的歌词。专辑中的 12 首歌曲，有 11 首半是迪伦的原创作品。其中，《答案在风中飘》成为 20 世纪 60 年代的时代标志曲和世界名歌。《暴雨将至》《战争大师》《北国姑娘》《别多想了，没事了》被认为是迪伦最佳作品、20 世纪 60 年代民谣经典，至今仍是迪伦现场表演的核心曲目。

　　从当时许多事情的迹象看，1962 年对迪伦来说并不乐观。首张专辑《鲍勃·迪伦》仅售出了 5000 张，单曲石沉大海，东家在郑重地考虑是否与他解除合约。迪伦能发表第 2 张专辑，全仰赖制作人哈蒙德和公司内大牌艺人约翰尼·卡什（Johnny Cash）的力挺。

　　该专辑录制于 1962 年 4 月至 1963 年 4 月，跨度长达一年，前后共进行了 8 场录音，其间，专辑曲目不断被刷新、被颠覆，共计产生了 20 余首录制完成却最终未收入专辑的作品，反映了迪伦此时井喷般的歌曲创作状态。

据他自己说，曾经一个晚上就写出了 5 首歌；在地铁上、在咖啡馆里，无论在哪儿，甚至在与人谈话时，灵感都会冒出来。关于这些创作，迪伦曾表达"它们是客观的、非个人的"想法。在一次采访中他说："歌曲就在那里。它们本身就存在，只是等待有人把它们写下来。我只是把它们搬到纸上而已。我不做，也会有别人这么做。"

迪伦的歌词，包括了对正在进行的民权运动的关切，对冷战和全球核战争的忧虑，对歧视、迫害、暴力、冷漠、利己主义的抨击，也包括痛苦而又决然的情歌，以及超现实的自嘲、荒诞和幽默。部分歌词的概括力和前瞻性之强，像是对之后发生的社会重大事件具有预言性，最典型的是《暴雨将至》，像是对其后发生的古巴导弹危机具有阐释力。整张专辑丰富的意象、现代性的诗歌、富有想象力的音乐、自然不做作的气质，奇妙地捕捉到了 20 世纪60 年代的时代精神和美国气象，吸引了世界各地离经叛道的青少年的目光，也使迪伦成为激进的知识分子和渴望新的文化复杂性的新兴大学生受众的宠儿。

有评论家将迪伦创作中话题歌曲和政治歌曲的突然增加，与迪伦和苏西·罗托洛（Suze Rotolo，即专辑封面上的女性）的恋爱联系起来。罗托洛一家有强烈的左翼政治倾向。迪伦在接受采访时部分承认了这种影响。这场恋爱，也成为专辑中情歌创作的动力。这些歌曲中渴望、失落和告别强烈交织的情绪，反映了迪伦与苏西时聚时散的紧张关系。

1962 年底和 1963 年初，迪伦应邀出访英国，伦敦之行为《暴雨将至》《战争大师》《北国姑娘》《鲍勃·迪伦的梦》带来了灵感，也带来了英国传统民歌和凯尔特民歌的影响。同时，专辑中的其他歌曲，则继续保持对黑人布鲁斯和美国乡村音乐的关注。迪伦一方面继承古老的民间传统，一方面对这些传统进行现代化的处理。歌曲编排如同上一张，继续保持简约。除了《科琳娜，科琳娜》采用了民谣乐队伴奏，其他所有歌曲都只有迪伦的自弹自唱，只使用了口琴和木吉他。

这张专辑是时事民谣创作的里程碑，具有文化、历史和美学的多重意义。它的成功使 22 岁的迪伦被媒体视为跨文化的重要艺术家，进而被称为"抗议歌手"和"一代人的代言人"，但迪伦否认了这些标签。

这一时期，迪伦表现出巨大的政治热情。他关心时事；频繁接触学生抗议组织；加入了民权运动；参加了1963 年 8 月 28 日的华盛顿大游行，呼吁消除对黑人的种族歧视。在林肯纪念碑下，面对 20 多万游行群众，迪伦演唱了《只是他们棋局里的一颗卒子》，彼得、保罗和玛丽（Peter, Paul and Mary）演唱了他的《答案在风中飘》，马丁·路德·金做了《我有一个梦想》的著名演讲。60 年代风云激荡，迪伦声名鹊起。

# BLOWIN' IN THE WIND

How many roads must a man walk down
Before you call him a man?
Yes, 'n' how many seas must a white dove sail
Before she sleeps in the sand?
Yes, 'n' how many times must the cannonballs fly
Before they're forever banned?
The answer, my friend, is blowin' in the wind
The answer is blowin' in the wind

How many years can a mountain exist
Before it's washed to the sea?
Yes, 'n' how many years can some people exist
Before they're allowed to be free?
Yes, 'n' how many times can a man turn his head
Pretending he just doesn't see?
The answer, my friend, is blowin' in the wind
The answer is blowin' in the wind

How many times must a man look up
Before he can see the sky?
Yes, 'n' how many ears must one man have
Before he can hear people cry?

## 答案在风中飘

一个人要走多少路
你才会称他人?
是啊,白鸽要越过几重海
才能在沙滩上睡觉?
是啊,炮弹要飞过多少次
才会被永远禁止?
那答案啊,我的朋友,它正在风中飘
答案正在那风中飘

一座山能存在多久
才会被冲刷入海?
是啊,那人能存在多久
才会获准自由?
是啊,一个人能转多少次头
假装他什么都没看见?
那答案啊,我的朋友,它正在风中飘
答案正在那风中飘

一个人要仰望多少次
他才能看见天?
是啊,一个人要有多少只耳朵
才能听见人们哭喊?

Yes, 'n' how many deaths will it take till he knows

That too many people have died?

The answer, my friend, is blowin' in the wind

The answer is blowin' in the wind

是啊，需要耗费多少条性命
他才知道太多人已经死掉？
那答案啊，我的朋友，它正在风中飘
答案正在那风中飘

# GIRL OF THE NORTH COUNTRY

Well, if you're travelin' in the north country fair
Where the winds hit heavy on the borderline
Remember me to one who lives there
She once was a true love of mine

Well, if you go when the snowflakes storm
When the rivers freeze and summer ends
Please see if she's wearing a coat so warm
To keep her from the howlin' winds

Please see for me if her hair hangs long
If it rolls and flows all down her breast
Please see for me if her hair hangs long
That's the way I remember her best

I'm a-wonderin' if she remembers me at all
Many times I've often prayed
In the darkness of my night
In the brightness of my day

So if you're travelin' in the north country fair
Where the winds hit heavy on the borderline

# 北国姑娘

哦，如果你在北国集市旅行
那儿的风猛烈抽打着边境
记着代我问候住那儿的一位姑娘
她曾是我真心爱恋的人

哦，如果你去时大雪纷飞
江河冰封，而夏日已尽
请看她是否穿上了温暖冬衣
足以为她抵御呼啸的风

请帮我看她是否还留着长发
那长发是否还在她胸口翻卷奔涌
请帮我看她是否还留着长发
她的这个形象我忆念至深

不知是否她对我还有记忆
多少次我向上天求乞
在夜晚的黑暗中
在白昼的光明里

所以如果你在北国集市旅行
那儿的风猛烈抽打着边境

Remember me to one who lives there

She once was a true love of mine

记着代我问候住那儿的一位姑娘
她曾是我真心爱恋的人

# MASTERS OF WAR

Come you masters of war
You that build all the guns
You that build the death planes
You that build the big bombs
You that hide behind walls
You that hide behind desks
I just want you to know
I can see through your masks

You that never done nothin'
But build to destroy
You play with my world
Like it's your little toy
You put a gun in my hand
And you hide from my eyes
And you turn and run farther
When the fast bullets fly

Like Judas of old
You lie and deceive
A world war can be won
You want me to believe

## 战争大师

放马过来吧，你们这些战争大师
制造了所有枪械的你
制造了杀人飞机的你
制造了重型炸弹的你
躲在墙后面的你
躲在桌子后的你
我只想要你们知道
我能看穿你们的面具

什么事都不做
只制造了毁灭
你玩弄我的世界
就像它是你的小玩具
你把枪塞到我手里
然后躲开我的视线
转过身你跑得老远
当那子弹快速飞来

就像古时候的犹大
你们满口谎言
想让我相信
世界大战能打赢

But I see through your eyes
And I see through your brain
Like I see through the water
That runs down my drain

You fasten the triggers
For the others to fire
Then you set back and watch
When the death count gets higher
You hide in your mansion
As young people's blood
Flows out of their bodies
And is buried in the mud

You've thrown the worst fear
That can ever be hurled
Fear to bring children
Into the world
For threatening my baby
Unborn and unnamed
You ain't worth the blood
That runs in your veins

How much do I know
To talk out of turn
You might say that I'm young

但我看穿了你的眼睛
看穿了你的大脑
就像我清楚地看见水
流过我家下水道

你们扣紧了扳机
叫别人去开枪
然后你们退后看
死亡人数不断上涨
你们躲在豪宅里
任由年轻人的血
流出了躯体
被烂泥埋葬

你们抛出了最大的恐惧
甚至于令人
不敢让孩子们
来到这世界
因为恐吓我
未出世未取名的婴儿
你们不配拥有
血管中流淌的血

我能懂多少
敢如此出言不逊
你们会说我幼稚

You might say I'm unlearned
But there's one thing I know
Though I'm younger than you
Even Jesus would never
Forgive what you do

Let me ask you one question
Is your money that good
Will it buy you forgiveness
Do you think that it could
I think you will find
When your death takes its toll
All the money you made
Will never buy back your soul

And I hope that you die
And your death'll come soon
I will follow your casket
In the pale afternoon
And I'll watch while you're lowered
Down to your deathbed
And I'll stand o'er your grave
'Til I'm sure that you're dead

说我一无所知
可纵使我比你们年轻
却明白一件事
就算是耶稣也不会
宽恕你们的所作所为

让我问你个问题
你的钱真那么管用吗
它会给你买来宽恕吗
你认为那行得通吗
我想你终会发现
当丧钟为你而鸣
你赚到的所有钱
都赎不回你的灵魂

而我巴望你死
巴望你的死期快到
我会跟随你的棺木
走过那个灰白的下午
我还会看着你下葬
看你堕入你的墓床
我还会站上你坟顶
确定你的确已经死亡

# DOWN THE HIGHWAY

Well, I'm walkin' down the highway
With my suitcase in my hand
Yes, I'm walkin' down the highway
With my suitcase in my hand
Lord, I really miss my baby
She's in some far-off land

Well, your streets are gettin' empty
Lord, your highway's gettin' filled
And your streets are gettin' empty
And your highway's gettin' filled
Well, the way I love that woman
I swear it's bound to get me killed

Well, I been gamblin' so long
Lord, I ain't got much more to lose
Yes, I been gamblin' so long
Lord, I ain't got much more to lose
Right now I'm havin' trouble
Please don't take away my highway shoes

Well, I'm bound to get lucky, baby

## 在公路上走着

哦，我在公路上走着
手里拎着箱子
是的，我在公路上走着
手里拎着箱子
主啊，我真想念我的宝贝
她在一个遥远的地方

哦，你的街道变得空空荡荡
主啊，你的公路变得满满当当
你的街道变得空空荡荡
你的公路变得满满当当
哦，我是如此深爱着这个女人
这肯定会要了我的命

哦，这么久了我一直在赌
主啊，我已再没什么可输
是的，这么久了我一直在赌
主啊，我已再没什么可输
眼下我遇上了麻烦
求您别让我没了鞋子走路

哦，我一定会走运，宝贝

Or I'm bound to die tryin'
Yes, I'm a-bound to get lucky, baby
Lord, Lord I'm a-bound to die tryin'
Well, meet me in the middle of the ocean
And we'll leave this ol' highway behind

Well, the ocean took my baby
My baby stole my heart from me
Yes, the ocean took my baby
My baby took my heart from me
She packed it all up in a suitcase
Lord, she took it away to Italy, Italy

So, I'm a-walkin' down your highway
Just as far as my poor eyes can see
Yes, I'm a-walkin' down your highway
Just as far as my eyes can see
From the Golden Gate Bridge
All the way to the Statue of Liberty

不然我一定会拿命一搏
是的，我一定会走运，宝贝
主啊主啊我一定会拿命一搏
哦，来大海中央见我吧
让我们把这条破公路甩在身后

哦，大海带走了我的宝贝
我的宝贝她偷走了我的心
是的，大海带走了我的宝贝
我的宝贝她带走了我的心
她把它打包装进了箱子
主啊，她带它去了意大利，意大利

所以，我在你的公路上走着
尽可能走向我可怜的眼能看到的远方
是的，我在你的公路上走着
尽可能走向我的眼能看到的远方
从金门大桥
一路走到了自由女神像

# BOB DYLAN'S BLUES

Well, the Lone Ranger and Tonto
They are ridin' down the line
Fixin' ev'rybody's troubles
Ev'rybody's 'cept mine
Somebody musta tol' 'em
That I was doin' fine

Oh you five and ten cent women
With nothin' in your heads
I got a real gal I'm lovin'
And Lord I'll love her till I'm dead
Go away from my door and my window too
Right now

Lord, I ain't goin' down to no race track
See no sports car run
I don't have no sports car
And I don't even care to have one
I can walk anytime around the block

Well, the wind keeps a-blowin' me

## 鲍勃·迪伦的蓝调

哦，独行侠和唐托
一路打马前来
解决每个人的麻烦事
每个人的，不包括我
肯定有谁告诉了他们
我过得很不错

噢你们这些五分一毛的女人
头脑中空空如也
我爱着一个真正的女孩
主啊我将爱她直到我死去
快离开我的门和我的窗
马上

主啊，我不会进入任何赛道
不会看跑车飞跑
我没有跑车
也完全不想有
我可以走路，随时围着街区走

哦，风一直吹着我

Up and down the street

With my hat in my hand

And my boots on my feet

Watch out so you don't step on me

Well, lookit here buddy

You want to be like me

Pull out your six-shooter

And rob every bank you can see

Tell the judge I said it was all right

Yes!

在街上时起时落 [1]
帽子拿在手里
靴子穿在脚上
小心点，别踩到我

哦，瞧瞧这儿伙计
你想学我的样子是吧
拔出你的六响枪
看见银行就去抢
告诉法官是我说的这没关系
是的！

---

[1] 时起时落，原指走路的方向，字面上也有"上"和"下"的意思。
权作此译，表现迪伦那种随风飘荡的状态。

# A HARD RAIN'S A-GONNA FALL

Oh, where have you been, my blue-eyed son?
Oh, where have you been, my darling young one?
I've stumbled on the side of twelve misty mountains
I've walked and I've crawled on six crooked highways
I've stepped in the middle of seven sad forests
I've been out in front of a dozen dead oceans
I've been ten thousand miles in the mouth of a graveyard
And it's a hard, and it's a hard, it's a hard, and it's a hard
And it's a hard rain's a-gonna fall

Oh, what did you see, my blue-eyed son?
Oh, what did you see, my darling young one?
I saw a newborn baby with wild wolves all around it
I saw a highway of diamonds with nobody on it
I saw a black branch with blood that kept drippin'
I saw a room full of men with their hammers a-bleedin'
I saw a white ladder all covered with water
I saw ten thousand talkers whose tongues were all broken
I saw guns and sharp swords in the hands of young children
And it's a hard, and it's a hard, it's a hard, it's a hard

## 暴雨将至 [1]

噢，我的蓝眼睛孩子，你去了哪里？
噢，我亲爱的小孩，你去了哪里？
我爬过十二架雾蒙蒙的山
我跋涉过六条蜿蜒的公路
我踏进七座悲愁的森林
我面对十二片死亡的海洋
我深入墓园的腹地一万里
啊暴雨，暴雨，暴雨，暴雨，
那暴雨就要来临

噢，我的蓝眼睛孩子，你看见了什么？
噢，我亲爱的小孩，你看见了什么？
我看见一个新生儿周围野狼环伺
我看见一条钻石公路上面空无一人
我看见一枝黑树枝它在不停滴血
我看见一屋子的人手握着带血的锤子
我看见一架白色悬梯每一级都没在水里
我看见一万个空谈家他们的舌头已经烂掉了
我看见枪和利剑握住它们的是年幼的孩子
啊暴雨，暴雨，暴雨，暴雨

---

[1] 本篇由郝佳校译。

And it's a hard rain's a-gonna fall


And what did you hear, my blue-eyed son?

And what did you hear, my darling young one?

I heard the sound of a thunder, it roared out a warnin'

Heard the roar of a wave that could drown the whole world

Heard one hundred drummers whose hands were a-blazin'

Heard ten thousand whisperin' and nobody listenin'

Heard one person starve, I heard many people laughin'

Heard the song of a poet who died in the gutter

Heard the sound of a clown who cried in the alley

And it's a hard, and it's a hard, it's a hard, it's a hard

And it's a hard rain's a-gonna fall


Oh, who did you meet, my blue-eyed son?

Who did you meet, my darling young one?

I met a young child beside a dead pony

I met a white man who walked a black dog

I met a young woman whose body was burning

I met a young girl, she gave me a rainbow

I met one man who was wounded in love

I met another man who was wounded with hatred

And it's a hard, it's a hard, it's a hard, it's a hard

It's a hard rain's a-gonna fall


Oh, what'll you do now, my blue-eyed son?

那暴雨就要来临

还有，我的蓝眼睛孩子，你听见了什么？
还有，我亲爱的小孩，你听见了什么？
我听见雷鸣的声音，它发出一个警告
我听见海浪的咆哮能淹没整个世界
我听见一百名鼓手他们的手在燃烧
我听见一万种低语但是没有人听到
我听见一个人在挨饿，我听见许多人在大笑
我听见诗人的歌那诗人死在水沟里
我听见小丑的声音他在巷子里叫喊着
啊暴雨，暴雨，暴雨，暴雨
那暴雨就要来临

噢，我的蓝眼睛孩子，你遇见了谁？
噢，我亲爱的小孩，你遇见了谁？
我遇见一个孩子，身边是匹死去的小马
我遇见一个白人在遛一只黑狗
我遇见一个年轻女性她的身体在烧着
我遇见一个小姑娘，送给了我一道彩虹
我遇见一个男人他被爱所伤
我遇见另一个男人伤他的是仇恨
啊暴雨，暴雨，暴雨，暴雨
那暴雨就要来临

噢，我的蓝眼睛孩子，你现在要做什么？

Oh, what'll you do now, my darling young one?

I'm a-goin' back out 'fore the rain starts a-fallin'

I'll walk to the depths of the deepest black forest

Where the people are many and their hands are all empty

Where the pellets of poison are flooding their waters

Where the home in the valley meets the damp dirty prison

Where the executioner's face is always well hidden

Where hunger is ugly, where souls are forgotten

Where black is the color, where none is the number

And I'll tell it and think it and speak it and breathe it

And reflect it from the mountain so all souls can see it

Then I'll stand on the ocean until I start sinkin'

But I'll know my song well before I start singin'

And it's a hard, it's a hard, it's a hard, it's a hard

It's a hard rain's a-gonna fall

噢，我亲爱的小孩，你现在要做什么？
我要在暴雨降临之前走回去
我要走进最深的黑森林深处
那里人丁众多却两手空空
那里毒丸在他们的河流泛滥
那里山谷中的家园紧挨着脏湿的监狱
那里刽子手的脸总是深藏不露
那里饥饿是丑陋的，那里灵魂被忘记
那里黑是唯一的颜色，那里无是唯一的数字
而我将讲述它思考它谈论它呼吸它
在山顶上反映，让所有灵魂都看见
然后我将站上大海，直到身体下沉
但是我将更了解我的歌，在我开始歌唱之前
啊暴雨，暴雨，暴雨，暴雨
那暴雨就要来临

# DON'T THINK TWICE, IT'S ALL RIGHT

It ain't no use to sit and wonder why, babe
It don't matter, anyhow
An' it ain't no use to sit and wonder why, babe
If you don't know by now
When your rooster crows at the break of dawn
Look out your window and I'll be gone
You're the reason I'm trav'lin' on
Don't think twice, it's all right

It ain't no use in turnin' on your light, babe
That light I never knowed
An' it ain't no use in turnin' on your light, babe
I'm on the dark side of the road
Still I wish there was somethin' you would do or say
To try and make me change my mind and stay
We never did too much talkin' anyway
So don't think twice, it's all right

It ain't no use in callin' out my name, gal
Like you never did before
It ain't no use in callin' out my name, gal
I can't hear you anymore

## 别多想了，没事了

坐着寻思来由没用，宝
反正这已无关紧要
而坐着寻思来由没用，宝
如果你现在还不知道
雄鸡对着破晓啼鸣
你望向窗外，我已离开
你是我继续上路的原因
别多想了，没事了

打开你的灯没用，宝
那盏灯我从没看到过
而打开你的灯没用，宝
我在道路黑暗的一侧
尽管我仍希望你做些或说些什么
试着让我改变心意留下
不过我们从未有过太多话
所以别多想了，没事了

喊我的名字没用，姑娘
好像以前你从不这样
喊我的名字没用，姑娘
你的声音我听不见了

I'm a-thinkin' and a-wond'rin' all the way down the road

I once loved a woman, a child I'm told

I give her my heart but she wanted my soul

But don't think twice, it's all right


I'm walkin' down that long, lonesome road, babe

Where I'm bound, I can't tell

But goodbye's too good a word, gal

So I'll just say fare thee well

I ain't sayin' you treated me unkind

You could have done better but I don't mind

You just kinda wasted my precious time

But don't think twice, it's all right

一路上我都在思索和追问
我爱过一个女人，人们说她是个孩子
我给她我的心可是她要我的魂
但是别多想了，没事了

我在这漫长而寂寞的路上走着，宝
我要去哪儿，我也说不清
但是再见这个词太过美好，姑娘
所以我要说的只是珍重
我并不是说你对我无情
你本可以做得更好但我并不在意
只是你有点浪费了我的宝贵时间
但是别多想了，没事了

# BOB DYLAN'S DREAM

While riding on a train goin' west
I fell asleep for to take my rest
I dreamed a dream that made me sad
Concerning myself and the first few friends I had

With half-damp eyes I stared to the room
Where my friends and I spent many an afternoon
Where we together weathered many a storm
Laughin' and singin' till the early hours of the morn

By the old wooden stove where our hats was hung
Our words were told, our songs were sung
Where we longed for nothin' and were quite satisfied
Talkin' and a-jokin' about the world outside

With haunted hearts through the heat and cold
We never thought we could ever get old
We thought we could sit forever in fun
But our chances really was a million to one

As easy it was to tell black from white
It was all that easy to tell wrong from right

## 鲍勃 · 迪伦的梦

坐在西去的火车上
我睡思蒙眬休息了一会儿
做了个梦真让我伤心
梦见自己和我最初的几个朋友

泪眼半湿我凝望着那房间
朋友们和我在那度过了许多个下午
我们一起经受了多少风暴
笑着唱着直到黎明来临

靠着古旧的木火炉挂着大家的帽子
我们的话说了，我们的歌唱了
我们一无所求但是那么满足
谈论着戏谑着外面的世界

那不安的心历尽了冷暖
却从未想过我们会老去
我们以为能永远坐那儿开玩笑
但那样的机会真的是百万分之一

区分黑白非常容易
分辨是非也一样

And our choices were few and the thought never hit

That the one road we traveled would ever shatter and split

How many a year has passed and gone

And many a gamble has been lost and won

And many a road taken by many a friend

And each one I've never seen again

I wish, I wish, I wish in vain

That we could sit simply in that room again

Ten thousand dollars at the drop of a hat

I'd give it all gladly if our lives could be like that

而我们很少选择，也从来不想
我们在走的那条道会分崩离析

多少年过去了无影无踪
又有多少赌局输输赢赢
多少条路朋友们一一踏上
而我再没看见其中任何一人

我多想、多想，多想都是妄想
我们能再次坐在那房间里
要一万美元也毫不迟疑
我将欣然奉上，假如人生还像那样

# OXFORD TOWN

Oxford Town, Oxford Town
Ev'rybody's got their heads bowed down
The sun don't shine above the ground
Ain't a-goin' down to Oxford Town

He went down to Oxford Town
Guns and clubs followed him down
All because his face was brown
Better get away from Oxford Town

Oxford Town around the bend
He come in to the door, he couldn't get in
All because of the color of his skin
What do you think about that, my frien'?

Me and my gal, my gal's son
We got met with a tear gas bomb

# 牛津城 [1]

牛津城，牛津城
人人俯首躬身
太阳照不到地面
不要去牛津城

他去了牛津城
枪支棍棒一路紧跟
只因他的脸是棕色的
快快逃离牛津城

牛津城就在转角
他到了门口，却进不了门
都是因为他的肤色
我的朋友，你有何见解？

我和我女友，和女友的儿子
饱尝了一顿催泪瓦斯

---

[1] 这首歌讲述了 1962 年的一桩新闻事件：退伍兵詹姆斯·梅雷迪斯
在密西西比州牛津城（一译牛津镇）的密西西比大学注册，成为该
校首名黑人学生。梅雷迪斯注册前夜，校园发生骚乱，冲突中两人
死亡。

I don't even know why we come
Goin' back where we come from

Oxford Town in the afternoon
Ev'rybody singin' a sorrowful tune
Two men died 'neath the Mississippi moon
Somebody better investigate soon

Oxford Town, Oxford Town
Ev'rybody's got their heads bowed down
The sun don't shine above the ground
Ain't a-goin' down to Oxford Town

真不明白为何至此
哪儿来的回哪儿去吧

牛津城的下午
人人在唱一首悲歌
两个人死在密西西比月光下
最好有人快去调查

牛津城，牛津城
人人俯首躬身
太阳照不到地面
不要去牛津城

# CORRINA, CORRINA

Corrina, Corrina
Gal, where you been so long?
Corrina, Corrina
Gal, where you been so long?
I been worr'in' 'bout you, baby
Baby, please come home

I got a bird that whistles
I got a bird that sings
I got a bird that whistles
I got a bird that sings
But I ain' a-got Corrina
Life don't mean a thing

Corrina, Corrina
Gal, you're on my mind
Corrina, Corrina
Gal, you're on my mind
I'm a-thinkin' 'bout you, baby
I just can't keep from crying

## 科琳娜，科琳娜

科琳娜，科琳娜
姑娘这么久你去了哪儿？
科琳娜，科琳娜
姑娘这么久你去了哪儿？
我一直在担心你宝贝
宝贝，求你快回来吧

我有一只吹口哨的鸟
我有一只唱歌的鸟
我有一只吹口哨的鸟
我有一只唱歌的鸟
可是我没有了科琳娜
生活也就没意思了

科琳娜，科琳娜
姑娘，你在我心里
科琳娜，科琳娜
姑娘，你在我心里
我在想你宝贝
我忍不住哭泣

# HONEY, JUST ALLOW ME ONE MORE CHANCE

Honey, just allow me one more chance

To get along with you

Honey, just allow me one more chance

Ah'll do anything with you

Well, I'm a-walkin' down the road

With my head in my hand

I'm lookin' for a woman

Needs a worried man

Just-a one kind favor I ask you

'Low me just-a one more chance


Honey, just allow me one more chance

To ride your aeroplane

Honey, just allow me one more chance

To ride your passenger train

Well, I've been lookin' all over

For a gal like you

I can't find nobody

So you'll have to do

Just-a one kind favor I ask you

'Low me just-a one more chance

## 亲爱的，只求你再给我一次机会

亲爱的，只求你再给我一次机会
陪伴你左右
亲爱的，只求你再给我一次机会
和你为所欲为
唉，我已经走在了路上
一只手抱着头
我在找一个女人
她正需要一个忧心的男人
我只求你发发善心
再给我一次机会

亲爱的，只求你再给我一次机会
坐你的飞机
亲爱的，只求你再给我一次机会
坐你的旅行列车
唉，我四下里寻寻觅觅
像你这样的女孩
却一个也找不到
所以你必须帮忙
我只求你发发善心
再给我一次机会

Honey, just allow me one more chance

To get along with you

Honey, just allow me one more chance

Ah'll do anything with you

Well, lookin' for a woman

That ain't got no man

Is just lookin' for a needle

That is lost in the sand

Just-a one kind favor I ask you

'Low me just-a one more chance

亲爱的，只求你再给我一次机会
陪伴你左右
亲爱的，只求你再给我一次机会
和你为所欲为
唉，要找一个
没有男人的女人
就像是寻找
丢失在沙滩上的一根针
我只求你发发善心
再给我一次机会

# I SHALL BE FREE

Well, I took me a woman late last night
I's three-fourths drunk, she looked uptight
She took off her wheel, took off her bell
Took off her wig, said, "How do I smell?"
I hot-footed it . . . bare-naked . . .
Out the window!

Well, sometimes I might get drunk
Walk like a duck and stomp like a skunk
Don't hurt me none, don't hurt my pride
'Cause I got my little lady right by my side
(Right there
Proud as can be)

I's out there paintin' on the old woodshed
When a can a black paint it fell on my head
I went down to scrub and rub
But I had to sit in back of the tub
(Cost a quarter
And I had to get out quick . . .

## 我将会自由

哦，昨天深夜我带回一个女人
我七八分醉意，她看起来紧张
她脱下她的轮盘，脱下她的铃铛
脱下她的假发，问："我闻起来怎么样？"
我脚着了火……赤着身……
跳出了窗！

哦，有时候我可能会喝大
走路像只鸭，跺着脚像只臭鼬
都别害我，不要伤我自尊
因为我有个就在身边的小情人
（就在那儿
骄傲无比）

我在外面刷着老柴房
一罐子黑漆落到了头上
我下来又洗又擦
却不得不坐进浴缸
（花了二十五美分
而我得赶紧出去……

Someone wanted to come in and take a sauna)

Well, my telephone rang it would not stop
It's President Kennedy callin' me up
He said, "My friend, Bob, what do we need to make the
    country grow?"
I said, "My friend, John, Brigitte Bardot
Anita Ekberg
Sophia Loren"
(Put 'em all in the same room with Ernest Borgnine!)

Well, I got a woman sleeps on a cot
She yells and hollers and squeals a lot
Licks my face and tickles my ear
Bends me over and buys me beer
(She's a honeymooner
A June crooner
A spoon feeder
And a natural leader)

Oh, there ain't no use in me workin' so heavy
I got a woman who works on the levee

有人要进来蒸桑拿）[1]


哦，电话响个不停
是肯尼迪总统找我
他说："鲍勃吾友，为了国家繁荣我们
    该怎么做？"
我说："约翰吾友，碧姬·芭铎
安妮塔·艾克伯格
索菲娅·罗兰"
（把她们和欧内斯特·博格宁放一个房间里！）[2]


哦，我有个女人和我睡一床
她又喊又叫又嚷嚷
舔我的脸又挠我的耳朵
让我弯腰又给我买啤酒
（她是蜜月大师
六月情歌手
汤匙喂食专家
和天生的领袖）


啊，没必要工作得这么苦
我有个女人她在堤坝干活儿

---

[1] 这一段讥讽南部种族隔离政策，当时南部及边境各州规定，黑人必
    须坐公交车后排，并为白人让座。
[2] 头三个人物都是国外性感女影星，后面的一个是美国男影星。

Pumping that water up to her neck

Every week she sends me a monthly check

(She's a humdinger

Folk singer

Dead ringer

For a thing-a-muh jigger)


Late one day in the middle of the week

Eyes were closed I was half asleep

I chased me a woman up the hill

Right in the middle of an air-raid drill

It was Little Bo Peep!

(I jumped a fallout shelter

I jumped a bean stalk

I jumped a Ferris wheel)


Now, the man on the stand he wants my vote

He's a-runnin' for office on the ballot note

He's out there preachin' in front of the steeple

Tellin' me he loves all kinds-a people

(He's eatin' bagels

He's eatin' pizza

He's eatin' chitlins

抽水抽到水没到脖子
每星期都寄给我一张月兑支票
（她棒极了
是个民歌手
跟那个谁谁
像一个模子刻的）[1]

某星期某日稍晚时分
闭着眼睛我半梦半醒
追一个女人追到了山上
恰好防空演习正在举行
那是牧羊女小波比！
（我跳入核掩体
我跳上魔豆茎
我跳进摩天轮）

现在，台上那人想拉我的选票
他正以无记名投票竞选公职
他在尖塔前演讲
告诉我说他爱各种人
（他吃着百吉饼
他吃着比萨
他吃着猪肠

---

[1] 貌似在调侃迪伦自己的生活，以及靠唱他的歌曲出名的女歌手，这
    些歌手会给迪伦汇来可观的歌曲版税。

He's eatin' bullshit!)


Oh, set me down on a television floor

I'll flip the channel to number four

Out of the shower comes a grown-up man

With a bottle of hair oil in his hand

(It's that greasy kid stuff

What I want to know, Mr. Football Man, is

What do you do about Willy Mays and Yul Brynner

Charles de Gaulle

And Robert Louis Stevenson?)


Well, the funniest woman I ever seen

Was the great-granddaughter of Mr. Clean

She takes about fifteen baths a day

Wants me to grow a cigar on my face

(She's a little bit heavy!)


Well, ask me why I'm drunk alla time

It levels my head and eases my mind

I just walk along and stroll and sing

他吃着牛粪[1]！）


啊，若安排我到电视现场
我会调到四频道
一个成年人从淋浴间出来
手上拿着一瓶发油
（就是油头小子的那玩意儿
橄榄球先生，我想知道
你怎么看威利·梅斯、尤·伯连纳
夏尔·戴高乐
和罗伯特·路易斯·史蒂文森？）[2]


哦，我见过的最好笑的女子
是清廉先生的曾孙女
她每天大约洗十五次澡
想要我在我脸上种一支雪茄
（她重了一点点儿！）[3]


哦，你问我为什么老是醉
那让我头脑清醒心情放松
我就喜欢走着、溜达着、唱着

---

[1] 牛粪，又有"胡说""废话"之意。

[2] 这里提到的人物都是当时的名人，依次是棒球明星、男影星、法国
    总统、英国作家（《金银岛》作者）。

[3] 这一段疑为讥讽所谓"清廉"政客。

I see better days and I do better things

(I catch dinosaurs

I make love to Elizabeth Taylor . . .

Catch hell from Richard Burton!)

看到更好的日子，做出更好的事情

（我捉恐龙

我向伊丽莎白·泰勒求爱……

被理查德·伯顿暴打一顿！）[1]

---

[1]　伊丽莎白·泰勒和理查德·伯顿因拍摄电影《埃及艳后》传出绯闻，
　　引起了轰动，成为当时最热门的娱乐话题。

# WHATCHA GONNA DO

Tell me what you're gonna do
When the shadow comes under your door
Tell me what you're gonna do
When the shadow comes under your door
Tell me what you're gonna do
When the shadow comes under your door
O Lord, O Lord
What shall you do?

Tell me what you're gonna do
When the devil calls your cards
Tell me what you're gonna do
When the devil calls your cards
Tell me what you're gonna do
When the devil calls your cards
O Lord, O Lord
What shall you do?

Tell me what you're gonna do
When your water turns to wine
Tell me what you're gonna do
When your water turns to wine

## 你要怎么做

告诉我你要怎么做
当阴影出现在你门下
告诉我你要怎么做
当阴影出现在你门下
告诉我你要怎么做
当阴影出现在你门下
主啊，主啊
你会怎么做？

告诉我你要怎么做
当魔鬼叫你的牌
告诉我你要怎么做
当魔鬼叫你的牌
告诉我你要怎么做
当魔鬼叫你的牌
主啊，主啊
你会怎么做？

告诉我你要怎么做
当你的水变成酒
告诉我你要怎么做
当你的水变成酒

Tell me what you're gonna do
When your water turns to wine
O Lord, O Lord
What should you do?

Tell me what you're gonna do
When you can't play God no more
Tell me what you're gonna do
When you can't play God no more
Tell me what you're gonna do
When you can't play God no more
O Lord, O Lord
What shall you do?

Tell me what you're gonna do
When the shadow comes creepin' in your room
Tell me what you're gonna do
When the shadow comes creepin' in your room
Tell me what you're gonna do
When the shadow comes creepin' in your room
O Lord, O Lord
What should you do?

告诉我你要怎么做
当你的水变成酒
主啊，主啊
你会怎么做？

告诉我你要怎么做
当你不能再扮演上帝
告诉我你要怎么做
当你不能再扮演上帝
告诉我你要怎么做
当你不能再扮演上帝
主啊，主啊
你会怎么做？

告诉我你要怎么做
当阴影爬进你房间
告诉我你要怎么做
当阴影爬进你房间
告诉我你要怎么做
当阴影爬进你房间
主啊，主啊
你该怎么做？

# WALLS OF RED WING

Oh, the age of the inmates
I remember quite freely:
No younger than twelve
No older 'n seventeen
Thrown in like bandits
And cast off like criminals
Inside the walls
The walls of Red Wing

From the dirty old mess hall
You march to the brick wall
Too weary to talk
And too tired to sing
Oh, it's all afternoon
You remember your hometown
Inside the walls
The walls of Red Wing

Oh, the gates are cast iron
And the walls are barbed wire

# 红翼之墙 [1]

哦，收容者的年龄
我记得很清楚：
不小于十二
不超过十七
像土匪一样扔进来
像罪犯一样丢出去
高墙之内
红翼之墙

从肮脏的旧食堂
齐步走到砖墙
累得不想说话
倦得唱不了歌
哦，整个下午
你思念家乡
高墙之内
红翼之墙

哦，门是铁铸的
墙上有带刺铁丝

---

[1] 红翼之墙，设于明尼苏达州的少管所。

Stay far from the fence
With the 'lectricity sting
And it's keep down your head
And stay in your number
Inside the walls
The walls of Red Wing

Oh, it's fare thee well
To the deep hollow dungeon
Farewell to the boardwalk
That takes you to the screen
And farewell to the minutes
They threaten you with it
Inside the walls
The walls of Red Wing

It's many a guard
That stands around smilin'
Holdin' his club
Like he was a king
Hopin' to get you
Behind a wood pilin'
Inside the walls
The walls of Red Wing

The night aimed shadows

远离那栅栏
里面有电
它让人耷拉着脑袋
待在号牌里
高墙之内
红翼之墙

哦，祝你好运
去深空地牢
告别带你去隔离室的
木板道
告别那分分秒秒
它们以此威胁你
高墙之内
红翼之墙

好多狱警
微笑着站在四周
手握棍棒
仿佛是国王
想着在木桩后
逮住你
高墙之内
红翼之墙

夜晚瞄准阴影

Through the crossbar windows
And the wind punched hard
To make the wall-siding sing
It's many a night
I pretended to be a-sleepin'
Inside the walls
The walls of Red Wing

As the rain rattled heavy
On the bunkhouse shingles
And the sounds in the night
They made my ears ring
'Til the keys of the guards
Clicked the tune of the morning
Inside the walls
The walls of Red Wing

Oh, some of us'll end up
In St. Cloud Prison
And some of us'll wind up
To be lawyers and things
And some of us'll stand up
To meet you on your crossroads
From inside the walls
The walls of Red Wing

穿过道道窗棂
风猛烈抽打
让墙板歌唱
许多个夜晚
我假装睡去
高墙之内
红翼之墙

当雨哗哗打在
工寮的木瓦顶
夜的声音
使我耳鸣
直到警卫的钥匙
咔嗒嗒奏起晨曲
高墙之内
红翼之墙

哦，我们中有些人
后来进了圣云监狱
有些人
以律师之类的事收场
有些人会站起来
在十字路口与你相会
自高墙之内
红翼之墙

# WHO KILLED DAVEY MOORE?

Who killed Davey Moore
Why an' what's the reason for?

"Not I," says the referee
"Don't point your finger at me
I could've stopped it in the eighth
An' maybe kept him from his fate
But the crowd would've booed, I'm sure
At not gettin' their money's worth
It's too bad he had to go
But there was a pressure on me too, you know
It wasn't me that made him fall
No, you can't blame me at all"

Who killed Davey Moore
Why an' what's the reason for?

"Not us," says the angry crowd
Whose screams filled the arena loud

# 谁杀了戴维·摩尔 [1]

谁杀了戴维·摩尔
为什么，原因是什么？

"不是我，"裁判说
"别拿指头指着我
我是可以在第八回合叫停
那也许能让他逃过厄运
但是观众会嘘，我敢肯定
因为未值回票价
他不得不死这太不幸了
可我也有压力，你知道
不是我让他倒下的
不，你根本不能怪我"

谁杀了戴维·摩尔
为什么，原因是什么？

"不是我们，"尖叫声填满
赛场的暴烈观众说

---

[1]　戴维·摩尔（1933—1963），美国次轻量级拳击手，曾获世界冠军，
　　　1963 年在比赛中因头部受伤而死亡。

"It's too bad he died that night

But we just like to see a fight

We didn't mean for him t' meet his death

We just meant to see some sweat

There ain't nothing wrong in that

It wasn't us that made him fall

No, you can't blame us at all"


Who killed Davey Moore

Why an' what's the reason for?


"Not me," says his manager

Puffing on a big cigar

"It's hard to say, it's hard to tell

I always thought that he was well

It's too bad for his wife an' kids he's dead

But if he was sick, he should've said

It wasn't me that made him fall

No, you can't blame me at all"


Who killed Davey Moore

Why an' what's the reason for?


"Not me," says the gambling man

With his ticket stub still in his hand

"It wasn't me that knocked him down

"太不幸了，那天晚上他死了
但是我们只是想看场拳赛
我们并不想他死
只是想看到一些汗水
这并没什么不对
不是我们让他倒下的
不，你根本不能怪我们"


谁杀了戴维·摩尔
为什么，原因是什么？


"不是我，"喷着大雪茄的
他的经纪人说
"这不好说，不好说清楚
我一直觉得他状态很好
他死了，这对他妻儿太糟糕了
但如果他有病，他应该早说
不是我让他倒下的
不，你根本不能怪我"


谁杀了戴维·摩尔
为什么，原因是什么？


"不是我，"赌拳的人说
手里还捏着票根
"击倒他的人又不是我

My hands never touched him none
I didn't commit no ugly sin
Anyway, I put money on him to win
It wasn't me that made him fall
No, you can't blame me at all"

Who killed Davey Moore
Why an' what's the reason for?

"Not me," says the boxing writer
Pounding print on his old typewriter
Sayin', "Boxing ain't to blame
There's just as much danger in a football game"
Sayin', "Fistfighting is here to stay
It's just the old American way
It wasn't me that made him fall
No, you can't blame me at all"

Who killed Davey Moore
Why an' what's the reason for?

"Not me," says the man whose fists
Laid him low in a cloud of mist
Who came here from Cuba's door
Where boxing ain't allowed no more
"I hit him, yes, it's true

我的手根本没碰他
我没犯什么丑陋的罪过
对了，我赌的是他赢
不是我让他倒下的
不，你根本不能怪我"


谁杀了戴维·摩尔
为什么，原因是什么？


"不是我，"拳击撰稿人说
一边在他的旧打字机上敲字
"不要怪罪拳击
橄榄球也一样危险"
又说："搏击由来已久
不过是个老美国的玩意儿
不是我让他倒下的
不，你根本不能怪我"


谁杀了戴维·摩尔
为什么，原因是什么？


"不是我，"那个用拳把他
捶进了一团迷雾的拳手说
他是从古巴来的
拳击在该国已被禁止
"是我打了他，是的，这是事实

But that's what I am paid to do
Don't say 'murder,' don't say 'kill'
It was destiny, it was God's will"

Who killed Davey Moore
Why an' what's the reason for?

但这是我受雇的工作
别说成'谋杀'，别说是'杀害'
这是命，是上帝的旨意"

谁杀了戴维·摩尔
为什么，原因是什么？

# SEVEN CURSES

Old Reilly stole a stallion
But they caught him and they brought him back
And they laid him down on the jailhouse ground
With an iron chain around his neck

Old Reilly's daughter got a message
That her father was goin' to hang
She rode by night and came by morning
With gold and silver in her hand

When the judge he saw Reilly's daughter
His old eyes deepened in his head
Sayin', "Gold will never free your father
The price, my dear, is you instead"

"Oh I'm as good as dead," cried Reilly
"It's only you that he does crave
And my skin will surely crawl if he touches you at all
Get on your horse and ride away"

"Oh father you will surely die
If I don't take the chance to try

# 七重诅咒

老赖利偷了一匹种马
可是被人抓住，押了回来
他们把他锁在监牢的地上
脖子上套着铁索

老赖利的女儿得了信儿
说父亲将被绞刑处死
她连夜策马清晨赶到
手里带着金子银子

那法官见到赖利的女儿
一双老眼在脑壳里陷得更深了
他说："金子不能救你父亲
亲爱的，你，才是那价码"

"啊我已是将死之人，"赖利哭道
"他想要的只是你
就算他碰你一下我都会毛骨悚然
快快骑马离开这里"

"啊父亲，若我不抓住这机会
你必死无疑

And pay the price and not take your advice
For that reason I will have to stay"

The gallows shadows shook the evening
In the night a hound dog bayed
In the night the grounds were groanin'
In the night the price was paid

The next mornin' she had awoken
To know that the judge had never spoken
She saw that hangin' branch a-bendin'
She saw her father's body broken

These be seven curses on a judge so cruel:
That one doctor will not save him
That two healers will not heal him
That three eyes will not see him

That four ears will not hear him
That five walls will not hide him
That six diggers will not bury him
And that seven deaths shall never kill him

付出那代价，不能照你说的
为了这点希望我得留在这里"

绞架的阴影令黄昏颤抖
夜晚猎犬狂吠
夜晚刑场呻吟
夜晚代价付出

次日早上她醒来
得知法官从未松口
她看见绞架弯曲
她看见父亲的尸体

送此恶毒法官七重诅咒：
一个医生医不好他
两名法师救不回他
三只眼睛瞧不见他

四只耳朵听不到他
五面墙壁藏不住他
六位墓工葬不成他
七次死亡也无法结果他

# DUSTY OLD FAIRGROUNDS

Well, it's all up from Florida at the start of the spring
The trucks and the trailers will be winding
Like a bullet we'll shoot for the carnival route
We're following them dusty old fairgrounds a-calling

From the Michigan mud past the Wisconsin sun
'Cross that Minnesota border, keep 'em scrambling
Through the clear county lakes and the lumberjack lands
We're following them dusty old fairgrounds a-calling

Hit Fargo on the jump and down to Aberdeen
'Cross them old Black Hills, keep 'em rolling
Through the cow country towns and the sands of old Montana
We're following them fairgrounds a-calling

As the white line on the highway sails under your wheels
I've gazed from the trailer window laughing
Oh, our clothes they was torn but the colors they was bright
Following them dusty old fairgrounds a-calling

# 尘土飞扬的老露天游乐场 [1]

哦，开春时即从佛罗里达北上
卡车拖车蜿蜒前行
像颗子弹射向嘉年华的路线
我们追随着尘土飞扬的老露天游乐场的呼唤

经密歇根的泥地过威斯康星的阳光
跨过明尼苏达边界，一路行色匆忙
穿越清澈的县湖和伐木工人营地
我们追随着尘土飞扬的老露天游乐场的呼唤

先到达法戈，再南下去阿伯丁
翻越古老的黑山陵，一路向前滚动
穿过一座座牛乡镇和老蒙大拿的沙地
我们追随着露天游乐场的呼唤

当公路的白线在你的车轮下飘
我从拖车窗户凝望、大笑
啊，我们的衣裳很破但是颜色鲜艳
追随着尘土飞扬的老露天游乐场的呼唤

---

[1] 露天游乐场，一种集市型的游乐场，临时组装搭建，在一个地方经
营一阵儿即拆掉转向另一个地方经营。

It's a-many a friend that follows the bend

The jugglers, the hustlers, the gamblers

Well, I've spent my time with the fortune-telling kind

Following them fairgrounds a-calling

Oh, it's pound down the rails and it's tie down the tents

Get that canvas flag a-flying

Well, let the caterpillars spin, let the Ferris wheel wind

Following them fairgrounds a-calling

Well, it's roll into town straight to the fairgrounds

Just behind the posters that are hanging

And it's fill up every space with a different kind of face

Following them fairgrounds a-calling

Get the dancing girls in front, get the gambling show behind

Hear that old music box a-banging

Hear them kids, faces, smiles, up and down the midway aisles

We're following them fairgrounds a-calling

It's a-drag it on down by the deadline in the town

Hit the old highway by the morning

And it's ride yourself blind for the next town on time

许多朋友随着那弯道转弯
玩杂耍的、骗钱的、赌博的
哦，我和算命师一类人一起消磨着时间
追随着露天游乐场的呼唤

啊，打下围栏，系牢帐篷
让那面帆布旗飘起来
哦，让"毛毛虫"[1]转圈，让摩天轮盘旋
追随着露天游乐场的呼唤

好，那就驶进镇子直奔游乐场
就在张挂着一排海报的后面
每一个空间都被各种不同的脸挤爆
追随着露天游乐场的呼唤

把跳舞女郎排在前，赌博节目压在后
听那老音乐盒砰砰响
听小孩子、脸、笑容在中间过道涌来涌去
我们追随着露天游乐场的呼唤

在镇子上盘桓直到结束时间
早上再驶上那条老路
闭着眼将自己准时载入下一个市镇

------

[1]　毛毛虫，游乐场中的旋转车。

Following them fairgrounds a-calling

As the harmonicas whined in the lonesome nighttime
Drinking red wine as we're rolling
Many a turnin' I turn, many a lesson I learn
From following them fairgrounds a-calling

And it's roll back down to St. Petersburg
Tie down the trailers and camp 'em
And the money that we made will pay for the space
From following them dusty old fairgrounds a-calling

追随着露天游乐场的呼唤

当口琴在寂寞的夜晚呜呜悲鸣
我们一边喝着红酒一边前行
我转过许多弯，学到了许多教训
因为追随着露天游乐场的呼唤

然后往回开去圣彼得堡
把拖车绑好了扎营
而我们赚来的钱将拿来支付场租
为了追随尘土飞扬的老露天游乐场的呼唤